The Strength Within

The
Strength
Within

FIND YOUR LIFE ANCHORS AND CULTIVATE
HABITS OF WHOLENESS, HOPE, AND JOY

Barbara Hansen

HiddenSpring

Cover and interior design by Cynthia Dunne

Library of Congress Cataloging-in-Publication Data

Hansen, Barbara, 1935-
    The strength within: find your life anchors and cultivate habits of wholeness, hope, and joy / Barbara Hansen.
        p. cm
    Includes bibliographical references.
    ISBN 1-58768-001-7 (alk.paper)
    1. Contentment. 2. Conduct of life. I. Title.
BJ1533.C7 H36 2000
170'.44—dc21   00-038839

Published by HiddenSpring
An imprint of Paulist Press
997 Macarthur Boulevard
Mahwah, New Jersey 07430

www.hiddenspringbooks.com

Printed and bound in the
United States of America

TABLE OF CONTENTS

To the memory of my parents, Ruth and Joe,
who gave me a jump start on my journey toward joy,
and
to my friend Rebecca Maureen,
who keeps me journeying in the right direction.

INTRODUCTION

L ife is lousy—at times. Life always will be lousy—at times. But when life is lousy most of the time, something is inherently wrong.

The bad news is that on any given day more people are battling loneliness and depression than are savoring satisfaction and joy. The good news is that it doesn't have to be that way. Because what's "inherently wrong" is largely internal, we often have the power to shape, mold, and change it.

If you sometimes wonder if life is worth living, if you often feel terminally alone, you may want to read this book.

It was written for anyone struggling to find meaning in the midst of a seemingly senseless life. If you're one of these people, I imagine there are days when you're sick and tired of going through the motions of this thing called living; days you're tired of being unappreciated, unloved, unneeded; days you hate getting up and facing another achingly empty twenty-four hours.

This book will not make your life problem-free. No book will. There will always be circumstances over which we have little control; life hands all of us dirty deals. Nevertheless, by taking the journey inward and knowing what's important, we can cultivate a sustained, rock-solid core of inner strength that stays with us even when things are not going well, through the ups and downs of daily living, even through those difficult times when life hands us dirty deals. *The Strength Within* will help you develop this inner strength.

You and I have a choice. We can stay stuck in a lousy, meaningless life, or we can walk toward joy.

Staying stuck is easy. Meaningfulness will always remain just a little beyond our grasp as long as our choices, actions, and attitudes are pulling in opposite directions from what we know is important. The strain of that pull creates a tension that causes our inner peace to fray, tear, and disintegrate. It rips our joy to shreds.

Walking on takes effort. Cultivating inner strength means gaining self-awareness, recognizing that who we are is more important than what we have, and knowing what qualities will help us become people we want to be. Without these rudders, these anchors, we float aimlessly through a meaningless life; with them we find every choice easier to make, every attitude easier to maintain. Rather than continue sitting in our own private pools of self-pity, we have the choice to begin cultivating inner strength.

This current book evolved as I listened to the hopelessness that permeates the lives of my students, friends, and readers. While promoting my last book *Picking Up the Pieces: Healing Ourselves after Personal Loss,* I became keenly aware that joy is hard to find. At book signings, radio talk shows, and interviews, I kept hearing: "People should read this book before a loss, not after. It prepares a person for living, not just for grieving." *The Strength Within* harvests some of the ideas that were only seeds in *Picking Up the Pieces:* suggesting ways we can overcome the hopelessness that creeps unwanted into our lives.

Having been a paraplegic for over forty years, I know life can be lousy. I also know inner strength isn't something we acquire; it's something we create. Gaining self-awareness and knowing what we value, we invite meaning into our lives.

Because no one can tell someone else how to live, I haven't tried. No one knows what hidden treasures and traps are strewn along someone else's journey through life. As you and I walk toward joy, we'll travel slightly different paths, but I've discovered while walking beside others making this journey that those paths are more parallel than perpendicular; they converge more than they dissect.

Much of the meaning that permeates my own life comes from my students, former students, readers, and workshop participants who have shared their lives with me. Their journeys have merged with my own, enriching both our trips and forming the nucleus of this book. Although the substance and details of the case histories given are authentic, names and identities have been changed to protect the confidentiality of friendship.

One of my major sources of joy is my friend Rebecca McDaniel, who cheers me on when life gets lousy, pushes me forward when hesitation paralyzes me, and claps wildly when joyful moments emerge. I want to thank her for having faith in my writing when my own faith wavered, for reading each chapter as the pages piled from the printer, and for editing every revision as carefully as if it were her own.

I especially want to thank Kathleen Walsh, my editor at Paulist Press, whose encouragement and support allowed this book to become a reality. Her keen eye for detail and organization has been invaluable.

If life is now lousy, I hope this book encourages you to take those first faltering steps toward a more meaningful life. I invite you to share with me your experiences as you travel the major highways, as well as the desolate detours, of your own private, personal walk toward wholeness, hope, and joy.

Barbara Hansen
University of Cincinnati—RWC
9555 Plainfield Road
Cincinnati, OH 45236

Get Ready:
Create the Foundation

BE AWARE OF OUR LIFE ANCHORS

AVOID TWENTY-FIRST-CENTURY OPIATES

QUIT PLAYING GOD

Man is the creator of his own happiness;
it is the aroma of a life lived in harmony with high ideals.

William George Jordan, *The Majesty of Calmness*

BE AWARE OF OUR LIFE ANCHORS

" I'm tired of living, tired of being unappreciated, unloved, unneeded. I'm tired of being alone, of being broke all the time. I don't have any close friends. Oh, people say they're my friends, but they're never there for me when I really need them. And I hate my job. No matter what I do, it's never enough and it's never appreciated."

Pausing to catch her breath, the woman continued, "I hate getting up each morning, hate facing another meaning-less, empty twenty-four hours. Each day I'm just filling up time; this isn't living."

This stream of frustration was being expressed by Denise, who had been my student and was now my friend. After thirty years of marriage, her husband had divorced her to marry another woman, leaving her with three grown children, little money, and an achingly empty life.

"This isn't living." The refrain was all too familiar. As I listened to the hopelessness in Denise's voice, I thought, "How often I hear those words." Clinging like a wet blanket, meaninglessness wraps itself around people's lives. Life seems senseless.

As students leave my English class and become my friends, I'm often the one they call when life turns rotten in their hands. Knowing I'll listen to the pain that's pounding their lives, they share with me the despair that often is kept carefully hidden from the rest of the world. Like other skeletons in the closet of their inner selves, this lack of joy is keenly felt, but seldom expressed.

> ◢ CLINGING LIKE A WET BLANKET, MEANINGLESSNESS WRAPS ITSELF AROUND PEOPLE'S LIVES ◣

Joylessness Permeates Many People's Lives

Many of the men and women I meet in my classroom, at book signings, at workshops, on radio talk shows, and in daily life share this despair. A similar thread of discontent weaves throughout many of our lives. Having experienced this despair and discontent myself, I'm well aware how difficult it is to throw off the blanket of meaninglessness that suffocates our joy.

You and I are so much alike that it's amazing.

How do I know we're alike? Because out of all the books lined on the bookshelf, you picked this one to hold in your hands. I know that for some reason your life is not as joyful right now as you'd like it to be. I'd guess there are nights you lie awake at three A.M., staring at the ceiling, trying very hard to find the strength to face the next day. Although life doesn't currently make much sense, you desperately wish it did. You're tired of the tearing pain and sorrow that penetrates your waking hours and pierces your dreams each night. You're sick of the emptiness, the loneliness, the hopelessness.

I know. I've been there. Over and over and over, I've been there.

This journey through life has stops we'd all just as soon not make, and I've had to make many of them. My first joy-destroying stop was on a dry, level Indiana highway over forty years ago.

A junior in college, an honors student, a leader in my youth group, decent-looking and popular, I was living a storybook life. Each day was a delightful gift to be unwrapped, savored, and enjoyed. Raised in a home filled with love and discipline, I knew I was adored, trusted, and appreciated. Given my parents' assurance that I could accomplish anything I set out to do, I joyfully plunged into life, attending classes, going on dates, and participating in church activities. Perched on the edge of adulthood, I liked the woman I was becoming—a woman whose hopes, aspirations, and dreams were now only inches from within her grasp. Joy saturated my soul.

This marvelous existence, however, came to a screeching halt on a hot, humid August afternoon in 1955. At nineteen, when my dreams were just beginning to crystallize, I was in an automobile accident that severed my spine and paralyzed me from the chest down. The joylessness that germinated on that late August afternoon was later to gestate and bring me perilously close to self-destruction.

Members of our youth fellowship group had been looking forward with eager anticipation to the events we'd planned for that fateful August Sunday. Each summer we took an all-day trip to some Indiana state park, tramping the trails, playing sports, and enjoying nature. Whether talking, teasing, or laughing, we teenagers embraced life with zest and passion; this picnic would be no exception. After leaving Muncie early on that Sunday morning and enjoying an all-day outing at Pokagon State Park, we had piled into cars and begun the two-hour drive toward home. But the five of us in our car never got there.

On a bright, beautiful summer day, our car and a car in the opposite lane slammed into each other, leaving two of my best friends dead, two others permanently disabled, and me, sitting in the middle of the back seat, paralyzed for life. In the months that followed, frustration, hopelessness, and despair became my constant companions. Handed a life I didn't want, and yet couldn't refuse, I began a journey that was to take me to hell and back.

This was only the first of numerous times when, like water pouring through a sieve, joy has drained from my life, leaving me trying to plug the holes and stop the pain.

Having experienced hopelessness and bitterness, I know how it feels to wake in the middle of the night and find suicide sitting temptingly on my shoulder. Having walked through this agony, I also know how it feels to discover that, much more than I want to admit, I determine the level of joy in my life. Paralyzed most of my life, I've found that life's lousy deals—in and of themselves—are not as significant as the inner strength we cultivate to deal with them.

When you woke this morning, were you haunted by a feeling of emptiness? Has your life become a seemingly senseless treadmill? Do you often feel terminally alone? Are there days you find yourself secretly wondering why you're living?

If so, you're not alone. Joy is hard to find.

We can't expect our lives to be free of loss, sorrow, or discontent —emotionally painful proofs we're human. Neither should we expect our lives to be an unending series of emotional highs. Show me someone who is continuously joyful, never admitting to life's lows, and I'll show you a person who is either a very good actor, mentally unstable, or hiding in busyness. Although we can't expect to have lives filled only with good times and glee, we can cultivate the inner strength to walk through the loss, sorrow, and discontent that periodically splatter joylessness all over our lives.

Beware of Temporary, Transitory Bursts of Joy

Genuine joy is in sharp contrast to the bursts of joy that flash like fireworks into our lives and then quickly flicker and fade away. When these magic moments occur—a benign biopsy report, a substantial raise, a passionate kiss—they're short-lived bursts of joy. Although spraying our lives with delight for hours, even days, we know they'll not last.

After coming through any unpleasant crisis, our present life seems wonderful when compared to that recent, rotten past. If we've just gotten out of the hospital where we weren't able to have normal bowel movements, had to use a catheter to urinate, and couldn't take a shower, when we' re home and have regained those simple, everyday abilities, life is good. If we've recently had a colonoscopy, waited with fear for the results, and then heard the doctor say, "Good news. Things look normal," life is good. If we've been jobless for six months and just signed a contract for a full-time job, life is good. For a few days, or even a few weeks, we savor that goodness. But try as we might to keep that euphoric feeling, it's going to slip away. Life's highs don't last.

Discovering that bursts of joy are transitory causes us to wring delight out of each moment they're with us. Knowing they are temporary intensifies our search for genuine, sustained joy.

I have these bursts of joy when people tell me I'm a good writer, an inspirational speaker, or an effective teacher. Having my twelve o'clock class discussion go well, receiving a loving phone call from a friend, or getting a long-awaited promotion all bring similar short spurts of joy into my life. Although very satisfying, I'm only too aware that these bursts of joy are temporary, fading out of my life as quickly as they dashed in.

Bursts of joy are not what this book is all about. The joy we're walking toward is a sustained, rock-solid, inner core of well-being that stays with us even when things are not going well, through the ups and downs of daily living, even through those difficult times when life is lousy.

Joy and Inner Strength Are Choices We Make

When drenched in joylessness, it's our tendency to feel helpless. We want answers; we want relief. We desperately want joy back in our lives. It's our choice, however, whether or not this happens. We can choose to cultivate the inner strength to walk toward joy, or we can continue wallowing in self-pity. Cultivating inner strength means taking a long, hard look inside our souls; it means asking and answering difficult, demanding questions concerning the inner self —questions we'd often just as soon ignore. Cultivating this inner

> ◣ CULTIVATING INNER STRENGTH MEANS TAKING A LONG, HARD LOOK INSIDE OUR SOULS ◢

strength means realizing that life is not gleeful, not a state of continual happiness; it means thinking, struggling, questioning, searching. To put it bluntly, it's hard work. But the earlier in life we start, the better.

To cultivate inner strength we need to know:

+ What's Important?

+ Who Are We?

+ What Inner Resources Count?

+ How Can We Create Inner Harmony?

When All Is Said and Done, What Matters?

Inner strength comes from knowing what's important. When some crisis knocks us down, we find ourselves—often for the first time in our lives—asking, "What's important?" Within the themes of classic literature lie the answers to what people throughout the ages have found to be "most important." Starting a unit on literature, I ask my students, "How is everyone in this room alike?" Without much prodding, they see that they all share similar needs: food, clothing, shelter, and health care. With some prodding, they become aware that they also agree on some universal core values. These values reach across race, gender, and socioeconomic status; they reach across the United States—from New York, to Cincinnati, to Los Angeles; they reach across continents, cultures, and centuries. These universal, never-changing values have stood the test of time. Literature reflects these values.

People throughout the ages have found *what's important is within them.* What's been true in the past is still true in the present. What's "most important" are those internal qualities that make us who we are, those qualities that strengthen our soul, qualities that are an outer reflection of an inner Spirit. Nevertheless, most contemporary teens, as well as many adults, are convinced what's "most important" is far different. Failing to recognize the universal truth that who we are is more important than what we have, they plunge into a life of acquiring and having, convinced something outside themselves will make them joyful.

When I ask my classes to list what's important to them, it's interesting that always, without exception, the students begin by listing money, possessions, and prestige. After putting on the board what they're suggesting as "most important," I tell them that we're all terminal. We simply choose to ignore the fact. I then ask, "When you're days away from dying, will having lots of money, the nicest home in the neighborhood, or an expensive sports car really matter?" Many realize it won't.

I continue questioning: "If you discovered tomorrow that you had only one more year to live, what would be important to you? When you're eighty and you look back on your life, what difference do you want your being alive to have made? What's really important? When all is said and done, what matters?" As I push them to think, discuss, and disagree, they realize there is a gap between what they're saying is important now and what they think will be important near the end of their life.

Who Are We? Who Do We Want to Become?
The crucial question becomes: "What do I want to *be*?" This is far different from "What do I want to *have*?" By knowing who we are, and more importantly, who we want to BE, we gain inner strength.

Self-awareness—the art of introspection, meditation, praying, and contemplation—shows with crystal clarity the value of *being* something, rather than having something.

Knowing who we are and who we want to become, we'll gain self-awareness. Patiently waiting and listening to that still, small voice within us, we grow more conscious of what's important. Gaining this awareness of what we want our lives to stand for demands that we simultaneously trust and test our thoughts, actions, attitudes, and choices. Each day becomes an opportunity for evaluating who we are and who we're becoming. While in the process of gaining this self-awareness, we find ourselves asking: "Is this thought my own or one I've blindly absorbed from my past? Will this action make a positive difference on those whose lives touch mine? Does this attitude enhance both my outer and inner worlds? Will this choice help me become the person I want to become? Do my thoughts, actions, attitudes, and choices reflect the inherent spirituality within me?"

Self-awareness requires silence and solitude. Peering into the hidden corners of the inner self requires concentration, quiet time, and privacy. It requires struggle and conflict. We soon see why Rollo May in *Man's Search for Himself* says, "For adults interested in rediscovering themselves, the search is centrally an internal one." This process of rediscovery of the self is done alone; it demands concentration. Identifying what's important and who we are demands our total attention. We'll find that we need noiseless time alone in order to get in touch with the inner self. Reflection, praying, and journal writing will help us, but only if we can let go of our need to control each and every moment of our life.

Although gaining self-knowledge demands solitude and silence, noiseless moments are hard to come by. Filling our days with

> FILLING OUR DAYS WITH CACOPHONY AND CLAMOR, WE EFFECTIVELY ESCAPE HAVING COMMUNION WITH THE INNER SELF

cacophony and clamor, we effectively escape having communion with the inner self. Yet, hard as it is, we must resist the noise that suffocates our thoughts and blocks our journey inward. Discovering the inner peace and benefits of silence, we soon agree with Thomas Merton when he says in *Love and Living*, "If we have no hope of being at peace with ourselves in our own personal loneliness and silence, we will never be able to face ourselves."

Realizing that our joy depends on knowing why we're living and what we stand for, we "face ourselves." In the safety of solitude and silence, we can peel off the layers of society's programming. This will mean giving ourselves permission to be alone, sitting on the deck, closing the door to our bedroom, going to the park, taking walks by ourselves. Creating these little slivers of solitude and silence, we'll discover what differences we want our being alive to have made. Slowly, thoughtfully, we'll know "what's important" and "who we want to become."

We live in a world starved for meaning. Realizing the barrenness of our lives, we grasp desperately for anything that will distract us for a few hours or days, making us forget how empty life is. Acquiring whatever we've grasped for, we inevitably find that it hasn't blotted out the barrenness. Meaninglessness persists. Joy will never be a part of our lives if we search for it outside the inner self.

What Qualities Will Help Us Become the Persons We Want to Be?

Each of us is currently practicing what John Powell in *Unconditional Love* calls a "life principle." He urges us to ask ourselves, "What do you really want out of life?" He says that each of us stakes his life on something, or someone, as the way to happiness. This "life principle" is very similar to what James Huber in *The Power of Personal Mission* calls our "core passion." Identifying our most important values is what Stephen Covey in *The 7 Habits Of Highly Effective People* means when he tells us to "begin with the end in mind" and be "principle centered." Whether we call it a "life principle," a "core passion," or being "principle centered," these core values rule our lives.

I call them my "life anchors." Because these anchors are within us, they're ours to cultivate and control.

Finding the core self, knowing what qualities will enhance that self, we'll discover our own personal answers to the crucial question, "What internal qualities will make me the person I want to be?" Because each of us is unique and individual, your life anchors won't be identical to mine; nevertheless, as we walk toward joy, we'll find that our anchors are more parallel than perpendicular; that they converge more than they dissect. Knowing our own personal life anchors gives an inner strength that will hold us solidly rooted in the midst of life's ups and downs.

Our life anchors will shift, change, and evolve as we grow in self-awareness. Because these anchors are what hold us firm when life tries to blow us off course, awareness of them is vital. Getting in touch with our core self requires self-discipline and tenacity. It also demands a constant juggling of our priorities. Knowing this, we'll think of self-awareness as an evolving process, not a static product.

We're searching for our souls—our inner, authentic, spiritual selves.

Life's Major Passages Shape Who We'll Become

I've discovered that with each new season of my life I repeatedly need to rethink and reshape my own personal life anchors, making sure I'm becoming the person I want to be, making sure my priorities fit this particular stage in my life.

For example, after my mother died sixteen years ago, I added "tenacious" as a quality I wanted to actively cultivate. One of my former professors suggested I think of the most positive quality my mother had possessed and consciously incorporate more of that quality into my own life.

It took only a few moments for me to decide my mother's strongest quality was her tenaciousness. She had an uncanny ability to stick with a situation, give it her best, and beat all odds. That tenacity gave her an inner strength few possess. As an accountant, during tax time she'd gotten up in the early-morning predawn hours to meet deadlines; as a mother, she'd unflinchingly faced and overcome the literal wreck that left me a paraplegic at nineteen and the figurative wreck that followed within my crushed soul; as an aging adult, she'd stared pain and death in the face when others would have given up years earlier. Because mother was now gone, there would be much less tenaciousness in the world. I therefore began to consciously develop and expand that quality within my daily life.

Similarly, when my father died eight years ago, I added "tolerance" as one of my life anchors. Although I admired him for a multitude of qualities, I knew it was his tolerance, his ability to let others live their own lives—regardless—that I admired the most. After pinpointing Daddy's most positive quality, I knew I had to put back into the world some of the tolerance that had been depleted with his death.

I'd been raised on his saying, "Every fool is entitled to make his own mistakes." I'd watched him allow people to be themselves rather than insist that they become clones of him; I'd loved him for letting me barge ahead, making my own choices, rather than telling me what to do, or worse yet, withholding his love if I didn't do exactly what he'd have chosen. With the wisdom of hindsight, I now see that his tolerance of my individuality allowed me to be free, knowing I'd never lose his love. What a rare and beautiful gift to give a daughter. Yes, the world was certainly going to have less tolerance now that he was gone. So I began consciously allowing my friends and relatives to "make their own mistakes," loving them even when I did not agree with their choices. Tolerance became stronger in my life.

Periodically rewriting and reaffirming my life anchors—actually putting words on paper—forces me to reevaluate why I'm living. Cultivating this awareness keeps me in touch with the person I'm becoming, helps me to live purposefully rather than drift aimlessly through life. If we fail to take what Dag Hammarskjold calls "the longest journey," this journey inward, we'll settle for a life buffeted by outside circumstances and other people's actions and attitudes. Rather than living life anchored in our own values, in our own spirituality, we'll dance around like puppets, pushed and pulled through life by whoever is currently holding the string.

How Can We Live in Harmony with Our Life Anchors?
When our attitudes, actions, and choices pull against our life anchors, our lives feel out of sync. Joylessness saturates our soul.

While walking through my own joylessness, and beside others floundering through theirs, I've discovered that the inner strength that results in sustained, genuine joy occurs only when we live in harmony with our personal life anchors.

Some of Us Take the Wrong Road; Others Get on a Detour

If our daily lives are not in harmony with what we believe is important, our choices may lead us down the wrong road or get us on a detour, reaching destinations that increase rather than decrease our joylessness. Lacking harmony between what we believe is important and how we live each day, we find ourselves swirled through life by the constant ebb and flow of transient emotions.

Many of us get on the wrong road because we've been repeatedly told by society that our joy will be in direct proportion to what we have/own/possess. Going down the wrong road can cause an unending internal struggle within our souls. Going down the right road, but ending on a detour, can leave us feeling empty and unfulfilled.

TAMMY TOOK THE WRONG ROAD AND FOUND FRUSTRATION

My student Tammy usually came into class a few moments late, always had trouble getting the assignments done on time, and often called to tell me she'd be absent that day. Reading an essay she'd written about how difficult it was to be both a mother and a student, I thought I finally saw the cause of her harried lifestyle. Having numerous students who are single mothers, I wrongly assumed that Tammy was one of them. After grading the essay, I turned to the last page and offered an invitation to stop in the office anytime she wanted to talk.

After the next class Tammy was sitting beside me, pouring out her frustration and concern. No, she wasn't a single parent. No, she didn't have to start college at age thirty-one. No, she didn't like her current life. "I'd give anything if I could go back to being only a wife and mother. Starting college has given me nothing but grief. I'm clinging by my fingernails to sanity," she sobbed.

"Why are you putting yourself through this pressure?" I asked. Tears streaming down her face, she answered, "Because Jonathan thinks I should. He says if I don't get a decent job, there's no way we can give the children a good life." Gaining assurance that Jonathan was her husband, I asked, "But what about you? What do you want?" "I want to quit college and be the best wife and mother I know how to be," Tammy quickly answered.

"Does your husband have a steady job?" I asked. "Oh, yes. He's an engineer at General Electric. But he says no one can live on only one paycheck these days," Tammy replied. Knowing they had sufficient money to live well, I continued, "What do you think? Is it financially necessary for you to get a full-time job now, while the children are in elementary school?"

"No," Tammy emphatically answered. "It's not necessary, but it's what Jonathan thinks is necessary. He wants our family to have all the toys and trinkets that the neighbors in our northeastern suburb have. He insists we look like them, act like them, and buy like them. We're doing that now, but Jonathan always wants more. We live in a $300,000 house, have more furniture and clothes than we need, and belong to the golf and swim clubs. But it's not enough. He wants his children to own better toys, wear better clothes, go to better schools. When they're teens, he'll want them to own better computers, have better cars, and go to better colleges."

We talked a long time that afternoon about values and life anchors. It became obvious to Tammy that the joylessness in her life resulted from her being out of harmony with what she believed was important. She was elated to discover that I didn't think she *had* to stay in college and thought her husband and she should talk to a psychologist about their differing life anchors; I encouraged her to list the internal qualities she wanted to strengthen. As we talked on the phone and at school during the remainder of the quarter, I slowly saw Tammy changing, accepting the reality that she had some control over her own life.

Believing that who we are is more important than what we have, Tammy was fighting an internal war. Realizing her actions were pulling directly against her life anchors, she quit college at the end of the quarter. She later told me that the best thing that came out of her short college experience was the conversations with me, the realization that she and Jonathan had to get some counseling. As a result, they started discussing their differences and weighing choices against their life anchors.

DIXIE TOOK THE RIGHT ROAD, BUT ENDED UP ON A DETOUR
While a student in my class, Dixie talked with me about her goals. After writing an essay concerning the qualities she was trying to develop in herself, she came into the office to talk. In the first year of the nursing program, Dixie was sure she'd taken the right road and said, "I'll have this neat opportunity each and every day of my life to practice being loving, empathetic, and a good listener, the qualities I wrote about in my essay."

We remained friends after she left my class, earned a four-year degree, became a registered nurse, and moved up the professional nursing ladder. One night she called nearly in tears. "Do you have any idea what it's like to have gotten a degree in a field only to discover it is nothing like you thought?" she lamented. I assured her that I did.

"Everyone thinks I'm this marvelous success story. The director of nursing stopped by today and told me that I'm a wonderful nurse. I'm not a nurse. I'm a paper pusher and a clerk," Dixie continued. "Every time I get a promotion or a raise, I'm moved a little further away from patient care. I don't even talk to a patient unless there's an emergency. And heroic as it may sound, rushing down the hall to handle an emergency is not why I became a nurse. I want to talk to patients, put my hand on their shoulder, listen to their fears, give them some attention. But, no, I'm either rushing from meeting to meeting or filling out mounds of paper work. I'm one of the highest paid nurses in the hospital, but I certainly have no joy," she sighed.

Gaining success in society's eyes does not always assure gaining success in our own eyes. Although Dixie was making more money than most of her friends, although she was pronounced successful by all who knew her, reaching the top, she'd looked around and found she'd sacrificed inner peace to get there. Society's success left her feeling empty, joyless, and unfulfilled.

Knowing that joy and inner strength occur as a result of who we are rather than what we have helps us make the needed U-turn and move our life focus away from "having" and back to "being."

Dixie made that U-turn, quit working at the hospital, and went into private-duty nursing, where she could live in harmony with her life anchors, where she could practice those qualities that would help her become the person she wanted to be.

Knowing Our Destination Makes the Journey Easier

Gaining awareness of what's important, we know what we want the final result of our life to be; we know our destination. We alone make the choice to develop, or not to develop, those qualities that will help us reach that destination. We can choose to cultivate or not to cultivate our life anchors. As a result of that choice, we can stand up to circumstances, or we can let circumstances toss us aimlessly through life.

But we know the choice is ours.

When we cannot find contentment in ourselves,
it is useless to seek it elsewhere.

La Rochefoucauld, *Reflections*

AVOID TWENTY-FIRST-CENTURY OPIATES

D iscontented, disillusioned, and despondent, we often face endless days when nothing seems right and everything seems wrong. Refusing to ask why we're living, we spend these days in mindless, purposeless pursuit of the trivial and the transitory. Life remains lousy.

Often a crisis slams us out of our despondency and into self-awareness. Perhaps your husband announces he wants a divorce; your mother is diagnosed with Alzheimer's; the boss tells us he no longer needs our services; a friend dies of a heart attack; a relative has a crippling stroke; or the biopsy shows possible cancer.

These are the moments when we're ripe for introspection. One of the few good things about life's dirty deals is that they force us to examine our priorities. There's nothing like a crisis to put things in perspective, to separate the significant from the trivial, to uncover what really is important in life.

Yet, many of us refuse to take the journey inward, fearing what we'll find.

Opiates Effectively Detour Self-Awareness

There are various reasons we avoid getting in touch with the inner self. For some of us, the trip is so painful that we'd prefer staying at home. Pinpointing what's important means we'd have to go into unexplored countries, examine frightening new territory, and travel unknown roads. Staying put is easier.

This pain of introspection is often stronger than our desire for joy. We keep the doors of our mind carefully barred, fearing to face what we've hidden inside. Refusing to cultivate the self-awareness of what's important, we find ourselves trapped in a joyless life. As Scott Peck says in *People of the Lie,* "We become evil by trying to hide from ourselves." Joylessness and despair can serve as the catalyst for tearing off the mask, but rather than confront those feelings hidden within, we fill our lives with distractions—distractions that effectively detour introspection.

I call these distractions twenty-first-century opiates.

Until we know why we're living, we're easy targets for these opiates. Never feeling centered, never feeling in sync, we flounder in meaningless circles. Watching these circles widen and grow deeper, we start searching for peace in all the wrong places. Wildly grasping for one of society's readily available opiates, we try to erase the inner pain rippling through our lives.

Rather than face the painful reality that's choking us, we blot it out. If one opiate doesn't work, we try a stronger one. We tell ourselves life will be better if only we can find the right opiate, the right distraction. Somehow, some way, we reason, we can eliminate unpleasant reality. We can't.

Failing to accept the reality that life has both pain and pleasure, wanting every problem to have a cure, we do everything possible to eliminate any unpleasantness that might creep into our lives. We reach for food, cigarettes, alcohol, or drugs; we turn on the computer, the television, or the VCR. Seeking to avoid joylessness, trying to avoid pain, we anesthetize ourselves with these opiates—opiates that society not only approves, but often applauds. Distractions abound. Escaping is easy. And many of us take the easy route.

Teaching the short story "Paul's Case," a story in which a boy's escapes get progressively worse, ending in the ultimate escape, suicide, I ask the students to list all the things in life that cause reality to be painful. They have no problem thinking of life situations from which they want to escape.

Then we make another list of all the ways people try to avoid this painful reality. Hands shoot up. Quickly the students compile a list of avenues people use to escape unpleasant reality. Their list goes from innocuous escapes such as sleeping, reading, and exercising to potentially harmful ones such as getting drunk, doing drugs, and committing suicide.

Turning to the board, I comment: "Obviously, these aren't all equally bad. What makes an escape healthy or unhealthy?" Pondering that for a few moments, someone usually decides, "How we feel after we've used it. If we feel worse than we did before, it's unhealthy." A student beside him agrees and says, "Yes, and some mess us up so much we can't even deal with reality, while others can be good for us." Another student raises her hand and adds, "How much we use it. Some of those things on the board are OK if used in moderation. Sleeping is a healthy escape, but if we sleep all the time, it would become an unhealthy one." Suddenly it becomes clear that an escape becomes an opiate, depending on how much and why we use it.

Many people believe that reality is more painful now than it was in the past and, therefore, contemporary society needs escapes and opiates in order to face this harsh reality. Having been a teenager during the late '40s and early '50s and a teacher of teenagers during the '60s, '70s, '80s, and '90s, I'm aware that outer reality is, has been, and will continue to be, difficult for all of us, regardless of which generation we were born into. The question isn't whether or not life will hand us dirty deals. It will. The question is whether we'll face them or hide in one of society's omnipresent opiates.

As our outer reality grows progressively more demanding, often we start opting for these opiates to fill the gaps and holes in the inner self. Although we quickly think of using drugs and alcohol to blot out reality and self-awareness, we often conveniently ignore three common opiates that our culture uses daily:

+ Television

+ Speed

+ Busyness

Filling our eyes and our ears with images and sounds from TV, our hours with distracting speed, our days with busyness, we effectively avoid strengthening the inner self.

First Tempting Opiate: Television

In the early '50s when television was a brand-new infant crawling into our lives, much was written about the possible effect this new addition would have on the human family. Articles, books, and classroom discussions were filled with debates concerning the influence TV would have on the soul of the viewer. Little did we realize how profound, how pervasive this influence would be.

Humans become what they hear and what they see. As we take the journey to self-awareness, when watching any show on television we'll find ourselves asking: "Is this program helping me become the person I want to be? Is it strengthening my life anchors?" Knowing that we become whatever we see and hear, we realize that the images and sounds of television stick with us, actually become a part of us.

For example, a promo for the show *Courtroom Drama* began with the words, "Power, Murder, Hate." The overvoice then asked: "What more could you ask for? It's all on *Courtroom Drama*." The first time I heard the promo, I thought, "What more could I ask for? How about humility, health, and love!" Listening and watching, I found myself asking, "Are power, murder, and hate going to help me become the person I want to be when they are the antithesis of the qualities I want to possess?"

Only by constantly monitoring the images we're allowing into our minds will we know if we're using the television as an escape, or as an opiate. Listening and watching, the viewer who's trying to live in harmony with his life anchors often discovers he doesn't want these images as part of his inner self. And he turns off the set.

We may, however, find turning off the set more difficult than we thought it would be. Although we easily see the addictive potential of alcohol or hard drugs, we have trouble admitting that television has the same potential. But it does.

If television is a daily part of our lives, we might try going for one day without turning the set on and watch our withdrawal symptoms. After going without the television for one day, perhaps we should try going without it for one week. This little test will give us a new awareness of the magnetic pull, the addictive potential of TV.

Although a delightful and effective escape from the stresses of life, most television programs are just that: an escape. Since escapes become opiates, depending on how much and why we use them, we see the power of this technological toy. If what we're watching isn't going to strengthen our inner selves; if what we're watching isn't going to nourish our souls; if what we're watching isn't going to help us live in harmony with our life anchors—we need to face the fact that we're using the television as an escape.

And all of us, periodically, need to escape. Now and then we need a refreshing break from the reality of life. If we're spending more hours escaping, however, than getting acquainted with our inner selves, television has become an opiate—an opiate that detours us from joy. Sedating our souls and numbing our senses, television effectively slams the door on self-awareness.

> ◣ SEDATING OUR SOULS AND NUMBING OUR
> SENSES, TELEVISION EFFECTIVELY SLAMS THE DOOR
> ON SELF-AWARENESS ◢

Second Tempting Opiate: Speed

Dash, dash; hurry, hurry. Rather than slow down and take the time to get in touch with why we're living, we rush headlong into life. Rushing becomes our normal pace—the pace of many of our days. On an unconscious or conscious level, hurrying has become our opiate. Speed rules our lives. By and large, society wants everything fast. For example, a few years ago when IBM brought out a new computer, the advertisement read: "A computer built for a world that needs everything done yesterday." This ad is symbolic of the speed that saturates our society.

I'm well aware how easily we can get addicted to an accelerated pace of living. When I moved from using a typewriter to a computer, I was in awe at the magic and the speed that this new toy brought into my life. But familiarity breeds acceptance, and finally contempt. Soon the computer's speed was taken for granted; with time it was even found lacking. After a few years of constant use, I'd catch myself impatiently waiting for the screen to appear between functions. When I upgraded that computer for a newer model, I watched in amazement as each screen appeared within seconds. After using the second computer for five years, this amazement turned into frustration. The speed I'd formerly delighted in now became a source of disenchantment. There was no doubt about it; this second computer was far too slow. So I bought a new computer, a faster one. And knowing the addictive nature of speeding through life, in a few years I'll likely find my current one wanting.

I was again reminded of the addictive nature of speed as I moved from an old printer to a new one. Many years ago after buying my first printer, I knew I'd discovered the most miraculous gadget ever made. After years of spending days at a typewriter retyping a chapter, here was this marvelous machine that would print it in minutes. I'd arrived. But when this plodding first printer wore out and was replaced by a new laser jet model, I could hardly believe how rapidly the new printer spit out the pages. By the time I went to the kitchen, got a cup of coffee, and returned to the study, an entire chapter would be lying in the tray waiting for me. And I loved it.

But there's a big difference between a person and a computer. While the Information Age is giving us marvels in some areas of our lives, it's also messing up our minds and our emotions in other areas. Faster is not always better.

> ◢ THIS PASSION FOR SPEED IS AN OUTWARD REFLECTION OF SOCIETY'S INTERNAL STATE OF MIND ◢

We rush through life, staying intellectually and emotionally disengaged from what we're doing—staying intellectually and emotionally disengaged from self-awareness. This passion for speed is an outward reflection of society's internal state of mind, a symbol of our refusal to take a long, hard look at our inner selves, to slow down long enough to contemplate what we want the final result of our lives to be.

If we doubt that we rush through life, we only need to test our own private pace. Testing our level of tolerance for doing things slowly can tell us a great deal about ourselves. For one twenty-four-hour period we can try to do each and every task slowly, methodically, and carefully. We can consciously, for that one twenty-four-hour period, slow the pace of our lives. We can talk slowly, walk slowly, and work slowly. We'll be amazed how this change of pace will be reflected in a changed attitude toward ourselves and toward life.

Third Tempting Opiate: Busyness

Keeping perpetually busy is another way we effectively keep self-awareness at bay. "I've got so much to do," we tell ourselves, "and so little time to do it in." By filling our date books with more than we can easily accomplish, we discover a readily available opiate—an opiate, unfortunately, that society applauds. Refusing to say no to any activity, we cram our lives full of engagements, appointments, meetings, activities, and tasks, leaving absolutely no free time in our busy schedule to get in touch with the inner self.

> ◢ Busyness blankets our pain ◣

In a life filled with picking up the kids, dropping off the cleaning, buying the week's groceries, dumping clothes in the washer, getting the birthday gift, changing oil in the car, meeting the boss, writing the report, scrubbing the toilet, attending the soccer games, paying the bills, planning the party, cooking the meals—we easily forget why we're living.

We may not realize it, but keeping perpetually busy, we avoid having to think. And thinking leads to self-awareness.

Are we depressed? Rather than feel the pain, we'll start a new project: Paint the bedroom, lay hardwood floor in the study, change the wallpaper in the kitchen. Are we sad? We'll spend weeks making a major purchase: research cars, refrigerators, or entertainment centers, visit showrooms, calculate and compare costs. Do we feel unloved? We'll enroll in that weight-loss program, take night classes, join the aerobic group. Busyness blankets our pain.

We often delude ourselves into thinking that our worth equals the number of activities we can squeeze into any twenty-four-hour period. Buying into this belief, we enmesh ourselves in a network of busyness, often juggling two or three tasks at one time. A woman drives her car, talks on the car phone, and puts on make-up; a man types a memo on the computer, sends a fax, and sorts the mail; a family watches television, talks to each other, and eats supper.

If we delight in making "to do" lists, make lists of our lists, feel we've accomplished nothing if at the close of the day we've not crossed items off those lists, and even write things down that we've done just so we can cross them off, we then know we're addicted to busyness.

If we find ourselves perpetually remodeling and redecorating the house, starting a new project immediately after we've completed our last one, buying new clothes before the old ones are worn out, replacing furniture when the current pieces are still in good shape, bringing a briefcase of work home with us each evening, juggling two or more jobs simultaneously—we know we're hooked on busyness.

If we can't tolerate "doing nothing," we need to understand why we feel this discomfort when faced with a day without projects, commitments, and meetings. If we have a low tolerance for life without a "to do" list, can't stand being alone for an entire day by ourselves—we're probably stuffing our life with busyness in order to avoid self-awareness.

An Awareness of Twenty-First-Century Opiates Helps Us Avoid Them

Gaining an awareness of which opiates we personally use to block out painful reality gives us power. Knowing our private opiates, our own Achilles' heels, we're in much better shape to control them.

Reaching for something outside ourselves for joy, we're going to be frustrated. Opiates are nothing but Band-Aids that we put on our discontent. And we soon learn that Band-Aids are only temporary coverings, not cures. Reaching for something outside ourselves doesn't work.

Once we know what we want the final result of our lives to be, we'll control the opiates rather than letting them control us. The more tightly attached our daily attitudes, actions, and choices are to our life anchors, the less need we'll have to numb ourselves with outer escapes.

Moving beyond the lure of these opiates is the beginning of inner strength. But it's only the beginning. If we stop there, without accepting the fact that we're not in total control of our life or anyone else's, we'll mistakenly believe that we have complete command of this person we're creating, absolute authority over what the final result of our life will be.

We don't.

To be sure, a human being is a finite being,
and his freedom is restricted.
It is not freedom from conditions,
but freedom to take a stand towards the conditions.

Viktor Frankl, *Man's Search for Meaning*

◢ 3 ◣

QUIT PLAYING GOD

Many New-Age thinkers would have us believe there is little in life we can't control. If we buy into their belief, joy will always remain just beyond our reach. We control neither the circumstances that come into our own lives nor the lives of those around us; pretending we have that kind of power weakens our ability to cultivate inner strength and walk toward joy.

We should not expect, nor strive for, a life without problems. The quicker we accept the fact that life is a balancing act, the more joyful we'll be. Living consists of an unending

> ⊿ JOY IS NOT BEING PROBLEM-FREE; JOY IS HAVING THE
>
> INTERNAL RESOURCES TO WALK THROUGH THE PROBLEMS ⊿

series of evolving circumstances, some delightful and others devastating. Joy is not being problem-free; joy is having the internal resources to walk through the problems.

Because it's so frightening to be at the mercy of circumstances, we often soak up whatever prevailing belief is being pushed in the current self-help books. Surely, we tell ourselves, by following the latest guru, repeating the correct mantras, and studying the prevailing trends, we'll gain control of our destiny.

When we do this, we're trying to play God. The only way we control our destiny is by cultivating life anchors, creating a steel core of spiritual strength that allows us to respond to the rotten circumstances that thrust themselves into our lives.

Although we know we're not fully free, we wish we were. In fact, at times we even pretend we are. But we're not. This frustrating fact is one of the major themes in the play *Oedipus Rex*, which lends itself to good class discussion. Asking the students if they agree with Sophocles that man is at both the mercy of his own actions as well as fate, I get solemn nods of agreement.

Relating this theme to our lives, we make two lists: "What things in life do we have little, or no, control over?" and "What things in life do we have some control over?"

We begin by listing all the ways people are "at the mercy of forces largely beyond their control." The students quickly come up with the fact that they had no control over who their parents were or what their environments were like for the first five years of life.

This, of course, leads to the fact that they also had no control over their genes, adding steam to the discussion as they list personal attributes over which they had no control.

Moving from genes to other uncontrollable forces, they decide that there are many circumstances in their lives that leave them nearly powerless. In quick succession, I hear things such as "death," "illness," "aging," "natural disasters," and "other people's actions." When the inevitable "other people's actions" is introduced, I always get a mixed response from the students. Only after some heated discussion do they admit that perhaps they don't have as much control over other people as they'd like to think they do.

We then move on to the other list, discovering, of course, that we have very little control over anything except ourselves.

We control neither circumstances nor other people, and pretending we have that kind of power weakens our ability to cultivate inner strength. By isolating what we can't control, we quit playing God; by isolating what we can't control, we take charge of what we can.

We Have Little Control over Circumstances

There are multitudes of circumstances that shatter our world to bits, circumstances that don't ask if they may enter our lives but simply barge in uninvited and unwanted. My students have the right idea when they mention death, illness, aging, natural disasters, and other people's actions as things that are "largely beyond a person's control." We have very little control over:

+ Coincidences
+ Illness and Aging
+ Natural Disasters

Most Coincidences Are beyond Our Control

Why am I a paraplegic? Not only have I asked myself that question over the years, but others have questioned me also. My answer is, "I was in the wrong car, on the wrong road, at the wrong time."

But society, by and large, doesn't want to believe that. Callers on talk shows have asked me if I believe I was in the wreck to make me stronger; participants at workshops have asked me if I believe I was in the wreck because I'd sinned. Hearing these questions for the first time, I was astonished. After fielding these questions for many years, I'm now aware that some people need to feel that nothing happens "by chance."

We so badly want to believe we have control of our lives that we tell ourselves if we are "good enough" nothing bad will happen—if something bad does happen, it will make us "good enough." Sorry, I just don't buy into that belief. Sure, I may in some way be a stronger person because I was paralyzed when I was nineteen. Sure, I may in some ways have sinned before I was nineteen. But I do not believe the wreck happened as a direct cause or result of either.

Bad things happen. Circumstances are not always what we want them to be. Given the choice, I'd not have lived most of my life in a wheelchair. But I wasn't given a choice. Being in the wrong car, on the wrong road, at the wrong time was a circumstance over which I had no control. I didn't ask for it, and I certainly didn't deserve it. But it happened.

Moving from normal nineteen-year-old to paralyzed paraplegic was not part of my life plan. Leaving my teens and entering adulthood, I was looking forward to being happily married, rearing secure children, and creating a loving environment for my family and those around me. Those plans crumbled that Sunday afternoon in 1955 when our car and another car slammed into each other, leaving me with my head split open and my spine cut in two.

After waking from a month-long coma, I slowly came to realize that my life would never be the same. Although I've never taken a step since that day, compared to all the other losses that were to be an inherent part of paralysis, this inability to walk was a relatively minor change in my life plan. Life had trapped me, stripping away all my freedom. I was at the mercy of my spinal cord, and I detested it. I hated not being able to make my body easily do what I wanted it to do; hated the fact that objects could no longer be easily carried, picked up, or moved; hated the helplessness that permeated every fiber of my life.

> ◢ BAD THINGS
> HAPPEN.
> CIRCUMSTANCES
> ARE NOT ALWAYS
> WHAT WE WANT
> THEM TO BE ◣

Wearing diapers and plastic pants each time I got dressed, giving myself an enema every other day to make my bowels move, sleeping on four towels each night to keep the bed dry were not exactly what I'd planned for my life. This inability to make my body do what I wanted was nearly insignificant, however, compared to the fact that two of my major goals in life had been snatched away from me: teaching home economics and building a marriage.

Six years after the wreck, I returned to Ball State University as a junior, switched my major from home economics to English, and started carving out a new professional life plan. Although I'd always had a passion for reading and writing, teaching English was certainly not what I'd originally planned for the rest of my life. Sure, I wanted to be a home economics teacher, but more importantly, I wanted to be a homemaker. Believing I could make the world a better place by being an effective wife and mother, when I started college I'd chosen to major in home economics. At the time of the wreck I had already completed two years of classes. Therefore, my move to English was much more than simply switching majors; it was an outward statement of an inward change that I found difficult to accept: Most likely I would not be a wife or a mother. And I rebelled at that reality with every fiber of my being.

But changing majors was to be a minor problem compared with all the others that were to barge into my academic life. Although I'd changed disciplines, I still wanted to be a teacher. My professors, advisors, and rehabilitation counselors, however, urged me to choose a safer profession. Teaching, all agreed, was not a wise professional goal for a paraplegic. Later I was to discover the cause of their concern: Indiana had never licensed a person in a wheelchair to be a teacher. But with my parents' encouragement, I, like Frost, took "the road less traveled" and was the first person in a wheelchair to be licensed to teach in the state of Indiana. After spending eight years taking classes, teaching both as a graduate fellow and an instructor, getting my B.S., M.A., and Ph.D. degrees, I discovered that being licensed to teach and being hired to teach were two very different things. Every educational door I tried to enter was either hopelessly stuck or slammed shut in my face. Knowing that teaching and I were meant for each other, I kept pounding on closed doors. In 1972 one of those doors swung open, and my new professional life plan was set in motion.

Getting a new life plan for my personal life, however, was even more difficult. As I watched my friends marry and start their families, I was keenly aware of the injustice of life. Yes, I wanted a husband; I wanted a family. But more to the point, I wanted to be first in someone's life. It didn't take many years for me to realize that one of my biggest losses was that no man would ever cuddle or desire me again. At twenty it was painful to realize that something so significant would not be a part of my future; at sixty it's painful to realize paralysis has denied me one of life's greatest pleasures.

On that day of transition from normal nineteen-year-old to paraplegic, my world shattered beyond recognition. And nothing I could have done would have controlled that day not happening. I was simply in the wrong car, on the wrong road, at the wrong time.

Illness and Aging Are beyond Our Control

Moving through the passages of life, we become keenly aware that illness, aging, and death are also beyond a person's control. It's true that each of us must take personal responsibility for his or her own health. In the final analysis, we choose what we put into our mouths; we decide how we're going to treat our bodies. Eating food that's low in calories and saturated fat; refraining from smoking cigarettes; abstaining from alcohol or drinking in moderation; getting enough rest and REM hours; practicing stress-reduction relaxation techniques; exercising thirty minutes three times a week—these are within our control. We also know, however, that we can do all of the above and, at some point, illness, aging, and death will still tromp into our lives. We're mortals with genetic limitations.

Older people become victims of illness and aging, trapped by circumstances over which they have no control. I watched that entrapment during the last year and a half of my father's life. After having a stroke, he entered the world of illness and health care centers, a world that forces people to become prisoners of their bodies' limitations as well as the rules of the center. Although in the very best health care center available in his city and receiving excellent care, he, nevertheless, was a prisoner, totally forced to abdicate all the freedoms that had been his for eighty-three years.

Within one day he went from a man who lived alone, attended concerts and plays, and traveled when and where he wanted, to being a helpless victim of circumstances. Loss of control was everywhere.

No longer could he start the day when he wanted. Here was a man who since retirement had stayed up late at night and slept in each morning until ten o'clock. Now he was being roused out of bed before six o'clock, pushed into the dining room while half asleep, and forced to stare at the walls and the other residents until breakfast finally arrived an hour later.

No longer did he have the privacy he'd always cherished. Now he was forced to share a room with another resident; let any aide that walked into that room rummage through his dresser drawers; allow social workers, relatives, and friends to read his mail. There were no hidden drawers, crevices, or corners where his private possessions or thoughts could be kept from the prying eyes of the world. Privacy was no longer an option.

No longer could he get out of bed or lie down when he wanted. Wanting to go to the bathroom during the night, he'd turn on the light and not get an answer. Following natural instinct, he'd try to get up, and then fall helplessly on the floor. Wanting to take a nap and asking to be put back into bed, he'd be told he needed to stay up because it "was good for him."

No longer did he have the freedom to relieve his pain. Needing medicine, he'd be told he couldn't have it—not because it was too soon, not because the doctor hadn't prescribed it, but because the nurse had decided it "wasn't good for him." Totally trapped in his new environment, he was helpless to make her follow the directives of his living will, which said he was to have pain medicine—even if it shortened his life.

These incidents were not the result of poor care; they were the result of illness and aging, two circumstances over which we have little control.

Natural Disasters Are beyond Our Control

Hurricanes, tornadoes, blizzards, and earthquakes do not tell us when they're going to arrive; they do not ask permission to enter our lives. They just crash in, unexpected and unwanted.

One crashed into my friend's life in April 1973. Attending an English conference in Anaheim, California, Rebecca and I were eating a leisurely breakfast before the morning session. Lost in the flowers, sunshine, and magic of Disneyland, we women from Ohio were oblivious to what was going on in the rest of the world. As Rebecca was paying our bills, I mindlessly glanced at the stack of newspapers piled on the floor by the cash register. The headlines stared at me: "Hundreds Killed in Midwest by Tornadoes." Hurriedly reading the story, it became evident that the two states hardest hit had been Indiana and Ohio. We taught in Ohio, and both our parents lived in Indiana. Panic set in.

Rushing to the phone, each tried to call her parents. Hearing my mother's voice, I gave a sigh of relief. "Yes," she assured me, "the tornadoes have wiped out towns all around here, but we're safe." During the day we repeatedly stopped at phones, trying to reach Rebecca's parents. No answer. By evening we were desperate.

After phoning every relative Rebecca could think of and getting through to none, we feared the worst. Although the worst had not occurred, neither was good news to be part of Rebecca's future. Her parents had left their home to go to town, seen the tornado cross the road in front of their car, and returned home to find devastation. The tornado had continued across fields and farms, clearing everything in its path. Her parents were safe; their home was gone. They had been on the receiving end of a natural disaster beyond their control.

At that time, both Rebecca and I thought we had experienced an awareness of what it feels like to be a victim of circumstances beyond one's control. We hadn't. Twenty-six years later on April 9, 1999, what had been only an awareness became stark reality.

Although my alarm was set for 6:10, for some reason I awoke at 4:50 that morning, got up, made coffee, and was starting my day when the civil alert sirens pierced the quiet of the predawn darkness. Because our sirens sound for both watches and warnings, I wasn't particularly worried as I sat in the bathroom of my home. Little did I know that a killer tornado was ripping across Cincinnati, heading into my life. Within moments, a deafening roar set my heart pounding. Putting the brakes on my wheelchair, clinging tenaciously to the edge of the sink, and praying for courage, I listened to my house crumbling around me. As the tornado violently swept through our neighborhood, destroying everything in its path, I experienced a fear unlike any I'd ever known.

When the roar ceased, I slowly ventured into the bedroom, feeling my way through the pitch blackness, trying to find the phone. Pulling up the shade by my bed, I stared in disbelief. Through the darkness I saw shells and shards of my neighbors' homes, uprooted trees toppled and twisted across cars, and acres of mature woods leveled to the ground. Lumber, shingles, and insulation filled the air. Flipping on the portable radio, I heard the announcer say, "The tornado has struck Montgomery and is heading northeast." Panic gripped me as I reached for the phone. Calling my best friend, whose home was in the path of the approaching twister, I breathlessly asked, "Rebecca, has your home been hit? Are you OK?"

Although houses only a few blocks from hers had been destroyed, she had no damage. "I'll be there as fast as I can," she assured me.

By the time I hung up the phone, neighbors were knocking on the door, checking on my safety, making me aware of the power of love. Although their own homes were gone, their possessions destroyed, and their lives shattered, they unselfishly walked through the rubble to be sure I was safe. As neighbors mingled in and out of my partially roofless home, hugging each other and crying in disbelief, the sense of caring and concern was poignant. For some unexplainable reason, I had the only working phone in the neighborhood. As people called loved ones to share the good news that they were alive and the bad news that their homes were gone, the predawn light showed with crystal clarity the stark devastation surrounding us.

Trying desperately to get to my home, Rebecca attempted three different routes, only to find each blocked by toppled telephone poles and mangled trees lying across streets. In desperation, she took a back road running parallel to Route 171, looked down and saw cars scattered on the interstate, flipped on their tops, twisted like Tinkertoys. Unable to get through the police barricade, she parked her car, and ran the rest of the way to my home. Adrenaline flowing and heart pounding, she arrived ahead of the disaster team. Once again, I saw the power of love.

Within less than an hour, the efficient and organized disaster team was in motion, searching the rubble for the injured and dead. A kind man came to my door and told me that I had to leave my condemned house immediately before any further structural damage occurred. Each of us living in the area was to go to the Red Cross clearing station already set up at the nearby high school. Listening to his gentle voice, knowing he wanted only to protect me, I was internally shrieking: "You don't understand. I can't leave my house. I must stay here. I'm paralyzed, I just got out of bed, and I'm not dressed. I don't have on any diapers, no plastic pants. I'm sitting on nothing but a rubber sheet and a towel, and I'll be urinating all over the place within an hour. I need catheters, urine bags, underclothes. I can't leave; you don't understand." But even as my mind was screaming with rebellion, I was reaching for my purse, stifling my fear, and, yes, I was leaving.

As I was being pushed up the hill toward the Red Cross station, surrounded by neighbors in robes and nightgowns, I felt a surrealism I'd never experienced before. Shocked and traumatized, my neighbors and I stared at the ruins in disbelief, trying to accept the unacceptable. Like robots, we headed toward the high school at the top of the hill. This couldn't be real.

I wasn't leaving just a house; rather, I was leaving my sole source of freedom. For most people, houses are just "stuff and things" and can be replaced. But for me, an aging paraplegic whose arms are wearing out, my house is my independence. The special features built within my home—those features that give me that coveted independence—could be replaced, but not for many weeks. And between now and then, I knew that I would be helpless, trapped by a body that refused to respond like it did when I was younger. No one except Rebecca comprehended that without the electric Barrier-Free lift that placed me in and out of bed and off and on the toilet; without the custom trapeze that allowed me to yank, tug, and pull my clothes on each morning while still in bed; without the special bathroom that allowed me to take care of my daily needs—I'd now be unable to function on my own.

Word quickly spread that two neighbors a block from my home had been killed. Wrapped in a blanket and sitting in the high school parking lot, I saw nearby a volunteer comforting and petting the dog of the couple who had died. Simultaneously, two of my former students were getting me coffee and comforting me as I coped with the rotten reality of no bladder control, no wheelchair van to get me to a hotel, and no home to live in. I felt a kinship with the mourning dog. Suddenly it was just too much, and I sobbed uncontrollably.

After five weeks of living in a hotel, I prepared to return to the building I'd left on April 9. This move back was greeted with, "Isn't it wonderful that you're going home?" Hearing that statement repeatedly, I wanted to scream: "No, it's not wonderful. I'm not 'going home,' for there is nothing but a house to go back to. It's a house that will give me independence, and that's wonderful. But you're ignoring the sense of rootlessness I'm experiencing. Before the tornado, I had a home sitting in a wooded haven, which nourished, nurtured, and sustained me. Those roots are no longer there. I feel as if I'm a transient, going to a 'motel' to live because that 'motel' is convenient, has in it all the things that make me independent. But it's not home."

I felt cheated. Yes, the house would be restored; however, the four acres of woods behind that house, the huge nature preserve beside it, and the deer, squirrels, chipmunks, possum, ducks, birds, and raccoons that lived there could not be totally restored for decades. Acres of towering, mature trees were gone. Difficult as it is, I'm still living with the losses spawned by this twisting, roaring wind which was totally beyond my control.

We Can't Control Other People

Another way we can quit playing God is to stop trying to control, manipulate, or change another person. Keeping our fingers out of someone else's life, keeping our minds open and our mouths shut, we accept the reality that we can't, we shouldn't, try to make someone into what we want her to be. If we want joy in our lives, we're going to stop making the rules for those around us, stop demanding they fit our mold, stop trying to run their lives.

Accepting a person "just the way she is," isn't easy when she fails to fit our criteria. But she not only needs but deserves the freedom to be herself. Why should we insist she be a clone of our expectations and our wishes? Loving her even when her looks, dress, habits, and personality don't fit our desires is one of the most difficult steps in cultivating inner strength.

> ❧ IF WE WANT JOY IN OUR LIVES, WE'RE GOING TO STOP MAKING THE RULES FOR THOSE AROUND US ❧

It's a step that becomes easier, however, when we let it sink into our souls how much we want others to accept us just the way we are.

Remember the first love of your life? Remember how wonderful it was to finally find someone who adored you just the way you were? When my students respond to an essay question asking them to describe the most significant person in their lives, before even grading the papers, I know one idea will be repeated in over half the essays: "She's the most significant person in my life because with her I can be myself. I don't have to fit her expectations. She isn't constantly trying to make me into what she wants me to be. It's wonderful."

Of course, maturity, marriage, and the passage of time will likely shatter that total acceptance. The first morning a wife finds her husband's coat and hat flung on the dining room table, his empty Coke cans and the remote control on the family room floor, and his dried cereal bowl sitting in the sink, the unconditional acceptance of dating may seem an illusion as it clashes with the reality of life.

But the fact remains that unconditional acceptance is what we all crave. We want our parents and spouses to love us even when our habits, dress, looks, and personalities aren't cookie-cutter replicas of theirs.

If we think we're going to change and control another person, we're chasing an illusion. Although we'd like to think differently, we don't have that kind of power. It's useless; it's selfish. It's the antithesis of love.

But when that person is our own son or daughter, it's hard. Wanting to make him into the person we'd like him to be, too often we relentlessly wield our control. Sometimes this control is blasting and blatant: "As long as you live in this house, you'll live by my rules." At other times, it's soft and subtle: "You've got such a pretty face that it's a shame you don't lose some of that weight." But both send the same message: "If you want my total acceptance, you'll have to twist yourself like a pretzel into what I want you to be."

In that atmosphere, joy walks out the door.

Jerome's mother was one of these unhappy, controlling people. When Jerome was my student, he told me that his mother had been upset that he'd chosen to major in music at a state university; she'd wanted him to major in business and go to a prestigious eastern school. And then he'd added, almost as an afterthought, "But then she wouldn't be pleased no matter what I did or where I went."

We kept in touch after he left college, went on to earn his M.A., got married, and started teaching at a school in another state. A gifted and talented musician, Jerome was respected in his field, praised by his peers, and liked by his students.

But his mother was determined to change him into the son she wanted him to be.

When Jerome was a teen, his mother tried to control his choice of friends, clothes, and career; when he was forty, her blatant control continued. On visits to his home, she criticized his friends, calling them uncouth and uncultured; bought him shirts, ties, and suits he never wore, pronouncing the casual clothes he liked as ugly and common; badgered him to cut his pony tail, saying she was ashamed to have her friends see him; tried to convince him to sell his small home, complaining that it lacked elegance and style. Nothing was right; everything was wrong.

Her message was always the same: "Look like I want you to look. Act like I want you to act. Live where I want you to live. Do what I want you to do." He waited for her to accept him as he was; she waited for him to fit the mold she'd created for him to crawl into. Neither had joy nor inner peace.

Brenda's control problem was different from Jerome's. In an essay, she told of her plans to get her degree in commercial art, work for a firm in Chicago, and "get a life of my own." But it soon became clear that her mother was doing everything possible to undermine those plans. Sensing how frustrated Brenda was becoming, I asked if she wanted to talk about the problem.

It wasn't hard to see that Brenda was unable to break free of a loving yet controlling mother. Divorced when Brenda was six years old, this woman had made her child the center of her life. As I listened I thought, "Her mother is terrified of losing her. Watching the center of her life slip slowly into adulthood, she's trying to keep the girl as attached and dependent as possible."

At the end of Brenda's freshman year, she gave up her hopes of being a commercial artist, dropped out of college, and became a clerk in a local department store, not because she lacked any artistic talent, but because she lacked the freedom to be herself.

Those conversations we started while she was my student continued for years after she left my class. With each phone call, I became more aware that her mother's control was subtle, but powerful. When Brenda got an offer to transfer to another job in a nearby town, Mother said, "No, dear, you'll be too lonely"; when Brenda bought her first car, Mother said, "I'll make your payments so you won't be pinched"; when Brenda commented that she needed new clothes, Mother said, "You don't have time to shop. I'll go to the mall today and buy you some nice things"; each time Brenda started seriously dating someone, Mother said, "You're such a help to me. I don't know how I'll ever run the house without you."

Even though Brenda was regularly seeing a psychologist, depression was her constant companion. Working at a job she didn't like, driving a car belonging to her mother, wearing clothes she hadn't chosen, staying single when she wanted to be married, Brenda felt like a nonentity.

One May evening she attempted suicide.

Each time we deny someone the freedom to create her selfhood, we diminish our own selfhood. Tolerance to openly, actively allow others to create their core self enriches us and makes us stronger. If we want to cultivate inner strength, we're going to give others the freedom to be themselves rather than insisting they become walking replicas of us. Failure to tolerate this freedom results in our attempting to play God with someone else's life.

Generation Gaps Increase the Temptation to Control

Having taught students during four different decades, I'm aware of the universal, never-ending generation gap that exists. Teaching in a college where 40 percent of the students are returning adults over twenty-seven years old, I have teenagers sitting beside men and women who often are old enough to be their fathers or mothers. As a teacher of this delightful age mixture, I'm able to see the generation gap "up close and personal."

One possible essay topic my students write on deals with the generation gap that exists in their families. Some of the strongest essays with the best specific examples are written by adult students whose children are married with homes of their own.

A grandmother who was a student in my class shared in one of her essays the frustration she always felt when visiting her daughter's home. Her comments are echoed repeatedly by other women whose grown children now have homes of their own.

Visits with her daughter's family were filled with ambivalence. One part of her knew the days would consist of enjoying her daughter, meeting new friends, and playing with her grandchild; the other part of her was aware that those days would also be filled with biting her tongue, hiding her dismay, and coming home totally exhausted.

She wrote, "Although I'm aware that as a parent of a grown child, I must back off, I find it difficult to stay in that house longer than four days. Their disorganization drives me nuts. It's impossible to find anything when I need it; clothes aren't put into drawers, food isn't put back into cupboards, clean dishes aren't even taken out of the dishwasher. They have no sense of organization, no plans, no timetable. Everyone just does his own thing, and no one really knows what's going on. They spend money like water, have no idea where it's going, and then complain constantly that they don't have enough to pay the bills. My grandchild calls her own shots and makes her own rules. She goes to bed whenever she wants, eats breakfast and supper in the family room while watching the TV, and leaves her toys and clothes scattered around the house. I love them dearly, but it's just more than I can take."

After grading the paper, I wrote her a note, telling her how often I read those same thoughts from other adults. As a result, she dropped into my office later to talk. I was impressed with her sincere desire not to control her grown children. Recognizing that they were living their lives differently than she was living hers, she was now desperately trying to give them the freedom they deserved. But it was hard; it was really hard.

As we talked, it became obvious to both of us that when people with two totally different perspectives on life are close relatives, something has to give. She really had only three choices: try to make them into what she wanted them to be, accept them "just the way they were," or break off the relationship. The first choice was useless, the second was difficult, and the third was unwanted. Dealing with this dilemma, she'd chosen to retain her own sanity and yet give them their freedom by limiting her visits to four days. Doing so helped both her and her daughter retain joy. Being tolerant of her daughter's lifestyle, even when it went against the grain, increased her own inner strength.

We Can't Control Whether or Not Someone Loves Us

To achieve inner strength, we must accept responsibility for our own emotions while realizing that we can't manipulate someone else's. We can be loving; we can be lovable. But when someone decides he no longer loves us, we must accept that reality without destroying ourselves in the process. We can't make someone love us. Love is not love unless it's freely given.

Margaret found this to be true. After twenty-nine years of marriage, one night her husband announced that he and her best friend had been dating for two years, had fallen in love, and were planning to be married. He'd already started divorce proceedings, and in his eyes, the only unfinished business was telling her and their four grown children.

His announcement that he no longer loved her, no longer wanted to share his life with her, took Margaret's breath away, surprising her beyond belief. Three years later, when she was a student in my class, she was still in a state of disbelief, still deeply in love with this man who had been her husband for twenty-nine years.

We became friends after she left my class, and I listened as she refused to accept reality. I watched as she tried desperately to win back his love. Telling herself that if she were only nice enough, pretty enough, generous enough, sexy enough, he'd see the mistake he'd made and return to her, Margaret turned her world upside down in an effort to control her husband's love. Of course, it didn't work. We can't make someone love us.

> ◣ WE CAN'T MAKE SOMEONE LOVE US. LOVE IS NOT LOVE UNLESS IT'S FREELY GIVEN ◢

During the twenty-nine years of their marriage, communication might have been created, feelings spoken, and love rekindled. It could have happened if both of them had wanted it to happen. But that was then, and this was now. It wouldn't happen now because only one of them wanted it to happen.

Love is a never-ending conversation. The monologue of trying to make someone love us will never replace the dialogue of love. As we loosen our grip on others' lives, we find we gain control of our own. As we encourage others to gain their selfhood, we grow more sure of who *we* are.

Control Is Not the Same as Influence

I've learned through personal experience, as well as the experiences of those around me, the futility of trying to make someone fit our desires and expectations. I'm convinced down to the core of my being that trying to control those we love quenches the joy in our own lives and in the lives of those around us. We gain inner strength when we practice tolerance and stop trying to control someone else's life.

Yet, by developing my life anchors, I'm hoping to make positive imprints on the people I come in contact with each day. And I'm a teacher. My lessons are based on behavioral objectives, specific ways I want to influence and change the students' skills, insights, or behavior. And I'm a writer. Each article and book is written because I want the lives of the readers to be enriched and changed.

So if my life anchors and my professions are these, how in the world can I profess that I'm not trying to control people? How can such opposing philosophies live harmoniously within me?

They can because *control* is not *influence*. There's a vast difference between controlling people and influencing them, and it's taken me a lifetime to discriminate between the two.

Influence occurs when someone helps us see ourselves more clearly, when someone creates an atmosphere in our lives that encourages us to change. But we do the changing. This atmosphere

is created by someone who will listen, affirm, and accept us—just the way we are.

Trying to make the world more pleasant, more positive, more meaningful for those I come in contact with each day, trying to give people the affirmation, time, and attention they need, I may or I may not influence them. My actions may or may not harvest change in another person. Influence is not control.

I'm changing the atmosphere; I'm not changing the person.

I know I've made a difference in people's lives. I have hundreds of notes and letters telling me that I have. But what small difference I may have made was not done by controlling; it was done by influencing. And that influence occurred because I tried to accept people "just the way they were"—flaws, wrinkles, and warts. That's not to say it was always easy. Many times I've been tempted, and often foolishly tried, to erase the flaws, iron out the wrinkles, or remove the warts. Attempting to do so not only was an exercise in futility; it lessened and polluted the atmosphere of my influence.

When we recognize that there will always be circumstances in our lives over which we have no control and that we can influence, but not control, other people, we quit trying to play God. Trying to pretend we have that kind of power warps our ability to respond to those circumstances. And that ability is what we're seeking.

Taking the journey toward self-awareness and accepting the fact we're not in total control of our lives or anyone else's, we've laid the foundation for wholeness, hope, and joy. We're now ready to cultivate the inner strength to face life's rough times. If life is lousy, we want to change it. And we can.

I've found that inner strength occurs as I strive to become more *tenacious, positive, loving, authentic, attentive, self-disciplined, and*

spiritual. These seven powerful, universal life anchors can help all of us create a sustained, rock-solid core of inner strength that stays with us through the ups and down of daily living, even through those difficult times when life hands us dirty deals.

Go:
Cultivate Inner Strength

STOP BLAMING OUR PAST

CONTROL OUR ATTITUDES AND HABITS

MOVE OUTSIDE SELF-CENTEREDNESS

ALLOW OURSELVES TO BE AUTHENTIC

LIVE LIFE IN THE NOW

PRACTICE DELAYED GRATIFICATION

CULTIVATE HOPE AND FAITH

Things that are done, it is needless to speak about...
things that are past, it is needless to blame.

Confucius

STOP BLAMING OUR PAST

Moving beyond the siren's call of the twenty-first-century opiates and squelching the temptation to play God, we hear with crystal clarity the discord and dissonance jarring our soul. Joy can't thrive when our days are spent pulling against our life anchors. Even as we're yanking and tugging, trying to pretend that our lives are meaningful, something deep inside us knows differently.

Facing this disharmony, we find ourselves asking: "What's the bottom line?" And we aren't referring to the bottom line of any profit and loss statement. When all is said and done, we discover that the only bottom line that counts is living in harmony with our life anchors. In order to become the person we want to be, we need to quit blaming our past and tenaciously take personal responsibility for our own lives.

Pop psychology, afternoon talk shows, and the current crop of self-help books have led us to believe that the emptiness permeating our souls is someone else's fault. Listening, watching, and reading, we may begin to believe that all our present problems originate from poor parenting or socioeconomic woes. Blame our genes; blame our gender. But, for goodness sakes, let's not blame ourselves!

Although society encourages us to blame past circumstances for present problems, doing so is a dead-end journey. In order to stop blaming our past and tenaciously take responsibility for our present, we'll want to:

+ Process the Pain of the Past

+ Choose Our Response to Reality

+ Stop Making Ourselves Victims

Process the Pain of Our Past

Katie, a returning student in her late thirties, was one of these people who found it difficult to stop blaming her past for every pitfall in her own life. In one of her essays, she told me that as a child she'd been sexually abused by her father. As I got to know her better, I discovered that regardless of what problem entered Katie's life, she quickly pushed the blame onto her "lousy childhood." She was a constant complainer, making a profession of self-pity. Part of the reason for this steady stream of dissatisfaction was that she'd never faced the pain of her childhood, never processed the anger. She was stuck in her past.

After leaving my classroom and becoming my friend, Katie would talk at length about her childhood, but she'd always say that she'd forgiven her father because "after all, no parents are perfect." Katie's constant shifting of the responsibility for her life onto her childhood, however, showed that she'd not really forgiven anyone; rather, she was hanging onto a past that, from her perspective, gave her a reason, a justification, for every problem she faced.

At my urging, Katie started talking with a psychologist. One evening after being in therapy for several months, she asked if she could come over and talk. Sitting on my deck, she seemed more relaxed than I'd seen her in a long time.

"I discovered one reason that I couldn't get on with my life was that I hadn't walked through the pain," exclaimed Katie. "First, I had to allow myself to remember, really remember, the hurt and humiliation I'd felt as a child. Then I needed to process that pain, both verbally and on paper. Finally I allowed myself to talk about how guilty, how dirty, how helpless I felt. At the beginning, I hated going to the sessions, rehashing the yucky stuff, bringing back the past. But telling the therapist how I felt then and how I feel now was like pricking this huge balloon inside me. The more I talked to her, the more the pressure lessened. And she encouraged me to continue those conversations when I'm at home, but to continue them on paper."

"You know," she continued, "you told our class that writing our feelings is therapeutic. Well, it is! I've written pages and pages to my father, pages I've torn up and trashed, but pages that helped me come face-to-face with my anger."

Katie finally accepted that the unpleasant reality of her childhood was not of her making; it was beyond her control. She came to realize it was OK to hate what her dad had done to her—to realize that although she couldn't change her past, she could tenaciously respond to it and take responsibility for the present.

Choose Our Response to Reality

Victoria and Kristin, two very similar women, had totally different reactions to the same situation: divorce.

I met these women a few years ago while they were my students. Both had entered college as a result of being divorced by their husbands. Both were in their late twenties, had two children, and lacked any skills to support themselves. For each, the divorce had been her husband's decision, not her own. But there the similarities ended. Whereas Victoria was devastated, having a terrible time accepting her new life, Kristin was doing rather well. This was the result of their differing responses to the situation.

Victoria's past had been one of satisfaction. As far as she knew, she and her husband had a good marriage. They had been active in their church, shared the fun as well as the responsibility of raising their children, and had never had any major disagreements. She'd been stunned when her husband announced he had been dating another woman for some time and now wanted a divorce. Her response was to crumble under the circumstances.

In contrast, Kristin's past had depended on the varying moods of her husband. Since the day she said, "I do," she'd been aware that her marriage was perched precariously on a shaky foundation. She'd overlooked her husband's mood swings because she loved him, delighted in being his wife. When he started dating another woman and demanded a divorce, she'd been shattered, but not destroyed. Her response was to tenaciously accept the circumstances.

Each of these women was forced into an unwanted divorce; both wished to stay married. But each chose to respond differently to her husband's decision. While Kristin quickly chose to be strong, it took years of therapy for Victoria to realize she had the same choice. Tenacious people like Kristin make a choice to live in the present, rather than cling to an unattainable past.

Rachel was another tenacious person who chose to take responsibility for her own life, even when that life didn't fit the stereotype her family approved. In an essay she confessed that it was a constant challenge to be single in a society that often equates marriage with success. At age thirty-six she had returned to college to complete her bachelor's degree. Although Rachel was currently living in Cincinnati, her family lived in rural southern Pennsylvania, where she had grown up. She wrote, "I hate going home for reunions and holidays. It's not that I don't like my family; I do. But with each trip, I must undergo interrogations by every aunt, uncle, cousin, and grandparent who sees me. It's always the same: 'Rachel, are you dating yet? How soon before you're going to settle down? Why are you still living in that huge city by yourself? Surely you want to have children, don't you?'" She later told me, "I feel as if I'm an outcast, and in some ways I am. My family, as well as most of their neighbors, are sure I'll never be a fulfilled person until I have a husband, kids, and a house with a white picket fence! They conveniently ignore the fact that I am leading a meaningful life, have great friends, love my job, and would rather be single than married to the wrong man. Because 'Mr. Right' has not appeared, doesn't mean I'm 'Miss Wrong'!"

Like Kristin, Rachel had made a choice to accept her life as it was rather than lament the fact that is wasn't what she'd anticipated when she was sixteen. She was well aware that her joy and self-worth did not depend on a man; they depended on her tenaciously taking responsibility to live in harmony with her life anchors. And she was doing just that.

Taking Personal Responsibility Creates Inner Strength

To walk toward joy, we must accept personal responsibility for our own bottom line. Personal responsibility, however, has gone out of style. Blaming our past for our present problems is easier than being tenacious—strong, tough, patient, and persistent.

Sure, some circumstances are rotten; sure, some situations stink. Past experiences are going to leave their stamp on us; we are the products of those experiences. They can't be denied; they can't be erased. They will forever remain a part of us. But at some point in time we must decide whether the past is going to rule us or whether we're going to take responsibility for how we respond to that past.

Because we choose how to respond, we are not pawns of a deterministic universe. You and I will always have the freedom of how we relate to the deterministic aspects of life. As long as a self-aware person has this freedom, he has inner strength. We see the truth of Rollo May's statement, "Freedom is involved when we accept the realities of life not by blind necessity but by choice." Tenaciously taking responsibility for our response to life's rotten deals is always our choice.

We all know people who have had difficult circumstances in their lives, have faced those circumstances, processed the pain, and made positive imprints on the lives of all they've touched. These people stand as inspirations for all of us.

Joseph Martin was one of these people.

The young life of Joseph Martin, son of immigrant parents who lived in rural southern Indiana, was filled with rotten reality. Trying

> ◢ TENACIOUSLY TAKING RESPONSIBILITY
>
> FOR OUR RESPONSE TO LIFE'S ROTTEN DEALS
>
> IS ALWAYS OUR CHOICE ◢

to find health and happiness, the family moved to Oklahoma when Joseph Martin was a baby. When he was two years old, his father died of cancer, leaving his mother to raise the boys. Six years later she moved the family back to southern Indiana. Never remarrying, teaching school, having little money, and living in a farmhouse with no electricity, no indoor plumbing, no central heat, and no marvelous modern conveniences, the widowed woman raised her two sons.

When Joseph Martin was fifteen and his brother was seventeen, their mother died of cancer, leaving them orphans. After her death, they lived alone in the farmhouse, doing their own cooking, cleaning, and farming. Knowing her death was imminent, his mother had asked a family friend to be the boys' guardian. Wanting guidance as to what "the rules" of his new life would now be, Joseph Martin went to his guardian and asked him what he could and couldn't now do with his life. The answer was: "Martin, your mother taught you right from wrong. You're to do right, and not do wrong." And with that wise advice, he set out into life.

From that day until he died at age eighty-five, he followed that advice. Graduating from high school the following spring at age fifteen, he entered college in northern Indiana that fall. Needing money to continue classes the following years, he decided he'd take the Indiana state teachers exam, teach winters, and finish his education during the summers. Although it was unusual for someone that young to take the test, not only did he pass the exam, but he missed only one question and was the first person to make a perfect score on the math section. This was the beginning of a life filled with similar experiences of success and joy.

Later during his life, he'd tell me, "If I were in school now, I'd be labeled underprivileged. If it were today, I'd be a boy from a broken home. Being raised by a single mother, I'd be considered an 'at risk' child.

He'd then continue, "But we didn't know we were underprivileged. All we knew was that now Mother was gone we had to make do on our own. And we certainly didn't know we were 'at risk.' It never entered our heads to blame anyone but ourselves for how our lives turned out. I'm glad I didn't know I was poor, at risk, and underprivileged!"

Poor and orphaned, this man entered college at sixteen, began teaching at seventeen, taught school in southern Indiana during the winters, attended college in northern Indiana during the summers, earned his B.S. and M.A. degrees, and then went on to become a sensitive and successful husband, father, friend, accountant, and teacher.

I know this is a true story, for Joseph Martin Hansen was my father.

Some would argue that it's harder for you and me to take personal responsibility now because our reality is so much worse than that of our parents. I doubt it. Yes, in some ways reality is worse in the twenty-first century than it was in past generations, but in many ways, reality is better. For example, technological and medical discoveries have increased the quality of all our lives. It's hard to label one generation "worse" or "better" off than the generations that came before or after. Physical pain, death, aging, loneliness, fear, rejection, and sorrow are constants of the human condition—regardless of which decade we're born into.

There are many men and women like Katie and my father, men and women from every generation, who have cultivated their internal resources, overcome difficult childhoods, and tenaciously faced life. There are also many men and women from every generation, like Kristin and Rachel, who have accepted life's realities and tenaciously moved forward. Doing so gave them inner strength and joy.

Stop Making Ourselves Victims

Some people don't realize our response to life's circumstances *is* a choice; they are convinced we are victims of circumstances. Tenacious people, I've discovered, are not victims. If we want to strengthen our inner selves, you and I must fight this victim mentality that currently permeates our society.

I see this lack of personal responsibility each spring quarter as college students "teacher-hunt." Moving from teacher to teacher, trying to find an easy grader, some students would rather teacher-hunt than learn the skills they lack. After moving into my class during spring quarter, receiving their first essay, and seeing that it earned an F, they often tell me it's my fault they received that grade because I "grade too hard," conveniently ignoring the fact that the rest of the class is doing passing work and that I graded everyone's papers using the same criteria. Being a victim of a teacher's grading is much easier than taking personal responsibility for lack of skills.

For better or worse, our past is a part of us. Taking responsibility for our response to the past prevents us from acquiring a victim mentality, a mentality that seriously detours the journey toward joy;

taking responsibility helps us get unstuck from our past. For years after becoming a paraplegic, I had to fight this victim mentality.

We don't choose the circumstances that walk unwanted into our lives, but we do, indeed, choose the response. This choosing can be seen in three totally different responses people give to the same regretful circumstance: paralysis. Some paraplegics give up inside and mindlessly, blindly follow society's existing rules for living in a paralyzed body. They invite meaninglessness into their lives, committing psychological suicide in the process. They are the living dead. A second group outwardly accepts the circumstances that have been given them, adjusting to what they believe other people expect them to be, becoming the "well-adjusted" paraplegics everyone applauds, while inwardly rebelling against the duplicity of their lives. These people don't die, but neither do they heal. The third group consciously confronts the fact that they hate the circumstances life has dealt them. Letting this hatred sink into their inner souls, they claw through anger, resentment, and pain. These tenacious people use this new rotten reality of paralysis for self-knowledge and inner strength. Believe me, it's easier to give the first or second response than it is to give the third.

> ◅ WE DON'T CHOOSE THE CIRCUMSTANCES THAT WALK UNWANTED INTO OUR LIVES, BUT WE DO, INDEED, CHOOSE THE RESPONSE ▻

After the wreck, I soon discovered that my life, as well as my spinal cord, had been split in two. From that moment on, time for me was either "B.W." or "A.W.": "before the wreck" or "after the wreck." For a long time, "B.W." was my wonderful past "A.W." was my unwanted present. Every aspect of living became colored by comparing it to how life used to be. I absolutely loathed the present and resented having it thrust upon me, unwanted and unasked. With an intensity that people can hardly imagine, I ached for the past that circumstances had snatched from me.

Life after the wreck was filled with frustration. Each new jolt of reality reminded me that my life would never be the same. New losses kept rearing their ugly heads, making me keenly aware of the sharp contrast between "then" and "now." And I passionately hated "now."

Picking up anything from ice cubes to essay tests when they slipped off my lap and onto the floor was always difficult, and often impossible. I'd repeatedly spend ten minutes pushing, pulling, and chasing a dropped bobby pin, pencil, or paper clip around the floor before I could finally position it for retrieval. Something as simple as dropping a bag of pecans and watching the contents roll around the kitchen floor brought frustration, anger, and self-pity. Watching the nuts lodge in dark corners and hidden crevices that I couldn't possibly reach, I'd resent the present state of my life and long for that wonderful past when I'd have easily and unthinkingly picked up the scattered pieces.

Suddenly I had no legs to help get me through the day. Everything—every stupid, dumb thing—had to be done with my hands and arms. No standing, no walking, no balance—it was just too much. Getting in and out of bed, off and on the toilet, and in and out of the car were now major productions, not automatic movements. Getting dressed was so much trouble and took so much time that I'd actually refuse invitations because I didn't want to make the effort. Having limited balance, pulling my skirt under me was difficult; fastening my bra became a daily comedy; and putting on hose required acrobatic skill. Daily living had become a series of hurdles to be overcome.

Needing my hands free to move my wheelchair, every movement, every activity had to be carefully planned, or I'd end up trapped somewhere, unable to move the chair and get where I wanted to go. Doing any messy task, I'd first place myself near the sink, so I could easily wash my hands. If I didn't, I'd find myself on the wrong side of the kitchen with pie, bread, cookie, or biscuit dough plastered all over my fingers. Life became a constant planning process. Spontaneity had gone out of my life.

Carrying anything on my lap became a perilous adventure: coffee spilled, vases tipped, hot casseroles burned. "No one understands," I'd think. "No one has a clue how hard my life is," I'd mutter. "Why me? I don't deserve this," I'd lament.

Discovering that my body no longer would do what I wanted it to do, I'd compare this horrid present to that terrific past when tasks had been so simple that I'd taken them for granted. Entering a new world that was filled with a constant craving for what was no longer mine, I found it easy to think of myself as a helpless victim of circumstances. This longing for a past that I couldn't retrieve was a painful yet necessary step in my healing process. Like every new passage in life, however, at some point that step must be transcended, not extended into a way of life.

The situations haven't changed; I've changed. I still hate being a paraplegic. Many days I'd like to hang a sign around my neck saying, "Life is hard. Please help me." I detest living in a body that makes every movement difficult. But rather than destroy today by aching for an unattainable past, I try to tenaciously respond to the present. Are there days I fail to be tenacious? You bet there are. But looking back over the past years of my life, I'm aware that I've lived best when I've tenaciously taken responsibility for the present.

If our past is worse than our present, we need to face and grieve for the loss of something we can never recover. Rather than bang our heads against a past we can't change, we'd do well to face the fact that our parents, siblings, or spouses failed to nurture us, failed to act as we wish they had. Once we admit to ourselves that the death, divorce, abuse, loneliness, poverty, or paralysis isn't fair, isn't just, and isn't deserved, then we can grieve the loss and move on.

In order to cultivate inner strength, however, we need to be tenacious—to be strong, tough, patient, and persistent. After we've ached with anguish, cried until no more tears will come, and hated with a passion those circumstances that have messed up our world, there comes a point in our lives when we need to say, "Enough is enough." Realizing that we can't change our past but can take responsibility for our present brings amazing inner strength.

The greatest discovery of any generation is that human beings can alter their lives by altering their attitudes of mind.

Albert Schweitzer, *Out of My Life and Thought*

◢ 5 ◣

CONTROL OUR ATTITUDES AND HABITS

Circumstances, in and of themselves, do not determine our destiny; to a large extent, we determine our destiny by our attitudes and habits. What we repeatedly think and do, we become. "Men imagine that thought can be kept secret," says James Allen in *As a Man Thinketh*, "but it cannot; it rapidly crystallizes into habit, and habit solidifies into circumstance." Attitudes are the building blocks, the foundation, of our habits and, therefore, need to be carefully monitored each and every moment of our lives. By changing our thoughts, our attitudes, we can modify our actions, our habits.

We gain inner strength when we purposely alter our attitudes and our habits.

We Control Our Attitudes

Monitoring and evaluating our attitudes, we're going to find ourselves asking: "Is this attitude enhancing or harming my spiritual inner core? Is it pulling me closer to or apart from my God? Is it strengthening or weakening my best self? Is it moving me toward or away from the person I want to be?"

Life consists of both attitudes and actions, but since our attitudes sow the seeds of our actions, they become our primary line of defense against joylessness. We control our attitudes when we:

+ Include the Verbs *Should*, *Must*, and *Ought* in Our Lives
+ Realize Our Attitudes and Our Feelings Are Not Synonyms
+ Practice the "Act As If" Theory When Having a Difficult Day
+ Accept the Fact That We're Two-Sided, Flawed Human Beings

Should, Must, *and* Ought *Are Needed in Our Vocabulary*
Asking ourselves, "Does this attitude strengthen my life anchors?" often leads us to discover that it doesn't; sometimes it's even counterproductive. At that point we should, indeed we must, consciously work to change such attitudes.

This idea that we *should, must,* or, *ought* to change our attitudes goes against the grain of all who have been bombarded with the belief that these three helping verbs need to be eliminated from our modern vocabulary. I believe, however, that *should, must,* and *ought*

> MONITORING AND EVALUATING OUR ATTITUDES, WE'RE GOING TO FIND OURSELVES ASKING: "IS THIS ATTITUDE ENHANCING OR HARMING MY SPIRITUAL INNER CORE?"

aren't the bad words that the past generations of self-help books have made them out to be. They've absorbed a negative connotation as a response to the fact that many people live their entire lives trying to be what others think they *should, must,* or *ought* to be. The key idea behind this belief that has permeated the psychology of the past three decades is that we'll never be emotionally healthy as long as we're living our lives to please others, ignoring our own needs in the process. And that's true.

Although it certainly is valid that we're healthier when we operate our lives out of our own priorities rather than blindly following our parents' or peers' priorities, we tread on dangerous ground when we eliminate *shoulds, musts,* and *oughts* from our lives.

If It's Going to Strengthen Our Life Anchors, Make It a Should
Our society has this tendency to take a very valid idea, discuss it to death, and then stretch it beyond recognition. The real question is, "*Why* do I feel I *should* do this?" "Does it grow out of my desire to fulfill someone else's expectations—at the expense of my own inner growth?" If so, hesitation is healthy; I probably should not do it. "Or does it come from my desire to strengthen my best self, to 'walk my talk'?" If so, I should do it. To take control of our attitudes, we'll want to make *should* part of our vocabulary. It's not bad or wrong to please ourselves—or to please others—if that pleasure results in strengthening our life anchors.

So what attitudes *should, must,* or *ought* to become part of one's everyday life? Therapists, psychologists, and self-help books don't have "the answer." I don't have "the answer." But you do. Any attitude that nourishes the soul and makes us better people should, must, and ought to be an essential, integral part of our daily lives.

Attitudes Don't Equal Feelings; These Words Are Not Synonyms

Once we've determined what we want the final result of our lives to be, we're ready to consciously create our attitudes. This is going to become difficult, however, if we aren't aware that attitudes are not the same as feelings.

Although our attitudes are closely related to our feelings, the words are not synonymous. Attitudes don't equal feelings. You and I don't have control of our feelings, and telling ourselves we do only leads to guilt and frustration. Feelings exist. We may feel fearful, loved, sad, lonely, angry, frustrated, or joyful; after all, fear, love, sadness, loneliness, anger, frustration, and joy are, and always will be, strands of the human condition. They are an inherent part of being alive. Although we can't eliminate our feelings, at any moment of any day we can alter our attitudes toward those feelings.

> ◣ ATTITUDES
> DON'T EQUAL
> FEELINGS ◢

Practicing the "Act As If" Theory, We Influence the Inner Self

Psychologist William James wrote that if we want a quality, we need to "act as if" we already have it. By "acting as if," we're able in an almost mystical sense to influence and create the quality we want. For better or worse, our attitudes influence our lives.

Try it. Keeping in mind the internal resources that will

strengthen your life anchors, think of a quality you want to possess. For one entire day, "act as if" you already possess that quality.

Let's say one of your life anchors is to be kind and loving. Even if you're feeling lonely and unloved, for one day "act as if" you are connected to people you meet. Think of someone you wish you'd talked with or written to, but didn't. Pick up the phone, pen, or paper; sit at the typewriter or the computer. Make that phone call; write that letter. Do it and you'll feel connected. Do it repeatedly, and you'll find communication and connectedness becoming an integral part of your life. It's true that we can change our lives by altering our attitudes.

We Two-Sided, Flawed Human Beings Have Some Lousy Times

But what if we're having a bad day, week, or month? Are we then failures if we can't "think ourselves happy?" Of course not.

But we feel like failures. If you're convinced, as I am, that we have control of our attitudes, you'll have, as I do, a very hard time allowing yourself to have down days. You and I feel guilty, blaming ourselves for not taking control of our attitudes. "I've failed," we tell ourselves. "If I'd only alter my attitudes, I could change my life."

And it's true. We could. But right now we can't.

Life Is Like a Yo-Yo

Like any good yo-yo, life has ups and downs. But we want life to have only the ups on the yo-yo. An effective yo-yo, however, goes both directions. For the ups on the yo-yo to be really high, it's got to have some equally low downs. We can't have life's breathtakingly beautiful highs without also experiencing some of life's lousy lows. Everyone has down times, bad days, rough periods, when nothing seems right and everything seems wrong. These down times simply remind us that we're two-sided, flawed human beings.

Although many of my friends and relatives have the illusion that I don't have down days, of course I do. When these days crash into my life, splattering sadness on everything they touch, I fight the fear that I'm being a hypocrite when I "act as if." And this fear punctures my inner peace each time I feel like staying in bed and pulling the cover over my head, but choose instead to get up, face the world, and be positive and pleasant.

Knowing my life anchors, however, helps me monitor my attitude during these inevitable down days. For that twenty-four-hour period, I consciously try to "act as if" I possess the life anchors I'm trying to cultivate inside myself. For example, when speaking to people during that day, I monitor my tone of voice, making it one that will encourage people to feel comfortable around me, conveying the reality that I care about them. When I close the classroom door and begin the lesson, I make a point to be upbeat, encouraging, and positive. Knowing that I'm consciously trying to live in harmony with my life anchors helps me handle these down days. I'm aware that I'm going to be a more effective person if I "act as if."

As these down days sometimes turn into down weeks, fear of being a hypocrite gnaws at my self-confidence, creating battles within my soul.

When my last book, *Picking Up the Pieces: Healing Ourselves after Personal Loss*, was reprinted in paperback, my father died a few weeks later. Simultaneously, I found myself promoting the new book, giving workshops, doing talk shows, and grieving for the loss of the most significant man in my life. Feeling alone, unloved, and unneeded, I questioned the honesty of giving motivational workshops. Who was I to be helping people deal with the same feelings that I was fighting daily! Fears of hypocrisy hovered over me.

A few months later, while working on this manuscript, I walked through additional sadness. Being an orphan was turning out to be much harder than I'd expected. Although I'd lived 130 miles from my parents for over twenty years, I saw them often, talked on the phone regularly, and wrote constantly. Their belief in me had always given an unwavering security that was no longer there.

Although I missed their emotional support the most, I also missed their physical presence. Even though they had lived in northern Indiana and I in southern Ohio, I knew that come "hell or high water" they'd be here if I needed them. The significance of being an orphan came barging into my life when my rotator cuff gave out not long after Daddy's death. With only good friends for my security net, I became aware how ALONE I now was in this world. For the three weeks my arm would not work, I had to depend on friends to lift me off and on the toilet and in and out of bed. Each night one of them would come over, put me in bed, and return the next morning to get me up. Spending those nights alone, immobilized in a bed I could not get out of, I became keenly aware I was now traveling solo through life.

No spouse, no children, no parents—it was just too much. Suddenly I was aware that in the dark, hidden crevices of my life there was a great deal of sadness. And I was writing a book on joy! The fears of hypocrisy not only hovered now; they pounded at me.

Am I being a hypocrite, a phony, if I "act as if" during these times? I think not.

I'd be a hypocrite if I put on a facade without knowing what I was doing; I'd be a hypocrite if I hid my feelings from myself and pretended that my life was "all honey and roses." A hypocrite would tell herself that "things really weren't too bad"; would not admit, face, and work through her pain; would run from reality rather than face it head on. A hypocrite would lie to herself. I don't do that.

I've learned that no matter what feelings are swishing through my life, I need to face them, feel them, and then release them. When I feel fear, sadness, or loneliness, I slow down, take a deep breath, and let myself hurt. Feelings need release, or they'll build up inside us, coming out in inappropriate ways at unexpected times. Crying, talking, and typing give form to my feelings, making this release easier.

Hurting is part of being human. Not facing and feeling that hurt is a big mistake.

But most of this hurting is done in private. I can be vivacious at school, during a book signing, or giving a workshop, but that doesn't mean that I have to be vivacious twenty-four hours each and every day. I can't; no one can. When I get home that night, I may very well fall apart emotionally, letting frustration take over as I type frantically and furiously, allowing tears to slide uncontrollably down my face.

We're always going to be what John Powell in *Happiness Is an Inside Job* calls, "a fraction." He says, "My act, my role, has been to make it look like I have it all together. It is very difficult for me to reveal my total self. I don't want people to know what a fraction I am." How true; how true. It should console all of us to realize that

> ◢ HURTING IS PART OF BEING HUMAN. NOT FACING AND FEELING THAT HURT IS A BIG MISTAKE ◣

we're not alone. Being flawed, two-sided human beings, we are, indeed, "fractions." As long as we face reality and are honest with ourselves, we are not being a hypocrite when we "act as if" in public.

The very fact that we flawed, two-sided human beings go *through*, and don't stay *in*, down times is proof that we're gaining inner strength; proof we're living in harmony with our life anchors; proof we're cultivating wholeness, hope, and joy.

We Control Our Habits

It's as easy to form a good habit as it is to form a bad one; which we cultivate is within our control. By choosing our habits, we create the inner self. The habits we hold today will make us the persons we'll become. If we think of what habits we want to possess when we're sixty, seventy, or eighty years old, we can begin practicing right now. As John Powell says in *Unconditional Love*, "In the twilight of our life our habits rule us. What you and I will become in the end will be just more and more of what we are deciding and trying to be right now." Whatever habits you and I are repeating today will be amplified at the end of our lives. If we're self-centered and negative when we're twenty, chances are great we're going to be intensely self-centered and negative when we're seventy; if we're caring and positive when we're twenty, chances are equally great we'll continue being caring and positive right up to the end of our lives.

We control our habits when we:

+ Realize the Power of Repetition
+ Make Positive Thinking a Habit
+ Choose Stimuli Wisely
+ Recognize That Our Comparisons Affect Us

The Magnetic Power of Repetition Can Give Us Healthy Habits
If we do anything repeatedly, it becomes a habit. We've all had experiences that prove to us how powerful habits can become, what a magnetic pull they have over our lives.

If we take the same route to work each and every morning, the car practically takes that route by itself. And then one morning when we want to go to the post office, not to work, habit takes over. We begin the trip on the same streets, but reaching the intersection where we must go straight to reach the post office, we turn automatically toward work. If we are distracted by something else, we follow the reflexes that are deeply carved by repetition.

When there's a power outage during a storm, we mindlessly reach for and turn on light switches, plug in and flip on appliances, even though we know on an intellectual level there's no current coming to the house. Hours into the power outage, we're still flipping light switches and trying to turn on the microwave and coffee pot. Habits are powerful.

Repetition of healthy choices creates good habits; repetition of unhealthy choices creates bad habits. But the choice is ours. Taking the time to develop an acute, conscious, never-ending awareness of what we're repeatedly thinking and doing, we're in a better position to create healthy habits—habits that will give us inner strength.

Positive Thinking Can Become an Acquired Habit
Negative thinking is a habit and, like any habit, it can be broken. It isn't going to get broken, however, without a conscious awareness of what we're doing. Since the easiest way to break any habit is to replace it with a substitute habit, negative thinking can best be lessened by habitually replacing it with positive thinking.

A positive attitude is not something we're born with. We create it—and we create it daily. We've all seen the same kind of situation destroy one person while making another stronger. And we've all asked, "Why the difference?"

I believe that problems are more likely to destroy people who have made a habit of letting themselves be destroyed, and to make stronger those who have made a habit of becoming stronger. A lot of life's responses grow out of habitual attitudes that we create, build on, and expand every moment, every hour, every day of our lives. By practicing, we can make our habits come from design rather than default. By looking for the good in the small, everyday, messy bumps life hands us, we find it. Later, when life hands us a mountain to climb, we look for the good, continue to find it, and successfully scale the mountain.

Like everyone else, I have numerous opportunities to control my attitude toward insignificant situations. This practice gives me proof that I can also control my attitude when life hands me a significant blow. For example, during the course of any school year, some student is going to question, sometimes challenge, something I've said in the classroom. At that moment I choose my attitude, and that attitude determines what my response to her will be. With repetition that response becomes a habit.

One response would be to show my dismay, cut her off, and shut her up. By my tone of voice, perhaps even by my words, I'd be telling her: "I'm the teacher. Don't you dare disagree with me." Another response would be to ask the class what they think, giving them the opportunity to agree or disagree with the student. With this response I'd be telling her: "You may have a good idea; let's see what others think." Or if I know she's got a good idea, a better idea than mine, I could admit it. With this response I'd be telling her:

"You're right. I'm wrong. Thanks for catching my mistake and making this issue clearer." Trying to live in harmony with my life anchors, I habitually choose the second or third response. Another teacher might respond differently to the same situation.

A vivid example of contrasting attitudes toward a similar situation occurred recently when a heavy ice storm and subzero temperatures closed all the major roads in Kentucky. During the storm, a local TV station interviewed people stranded in various shelters, people who had been waiting eight days for the main roads to be opened.

One delightful couple, who were on their way to Florida to celebrate their fiftieth wedding anniversary, were making the best of the situation. They'd made new friends at the shelter, bought a wedding cake, had their anniversary party with their new friends, and were having a pleasant time. In sharp contrast was a man who cursed the snow, the state, the roads, the shelter, and announced near the end of the interview that he'd "never set foot in Florence, Kentucky, again!"

As I watched the news broadcast, I thought, "Each response is probably typical of that person's general response to life." The couple had made a habit of looking for the good; the man had made a habit of looking for the bad. Each found what he was looking for. Positive thinking is, indeed, an acquired habit.

We Become What We See and Hear

What's in our mind makes us who we are. James Allen says in *As a Man Thinketh*, "A man is literally what he thinks, his character being the complete sum of all his thoughts." Our nervous system takes in the stimuli around us each and every moment. That stimuli makes our reality, and we can *change our reality* by changing our stimuli. Our environment is constantly pouring out sounds and images, but we control which ones we choose to let into our lives.

Proof is all around us that what we hear and what we see become a part of us. We've all watched a TV show, awakened in the middle of the night, and found swirling through our minds the plot of that show—a plot that wouldn't even be there if we hadn't watched that particular show. We've all had company for dinner, gone to bed later that evening, and lain awake replaying the events of the evening in our mind. Even in the middle of the night, we may wake up and go over the conversations that occurred—conversations that wouldn't even be in our mind if we hadn't hosted the dinner party.

We can make what we hear and see strengthen our life anchors when we:

+ Monitor Our Daily Environment
+ Make Deposits in Our Mind's Memory Bank

Monitor Our Environment

By filling our environment with peace, beauty, and calmness, by consciously choosing what we absorb each day, we can become the persons we want to be. Yet, often if we look carefully at each room in our homes, we find that the environment we spend the most time in does not feed our souls nor strengthen our inner peace. Rather, we may discover that our surroundings distract and deplete, making it difficult to achieve the calmness we crave.

Creating a home that nourishes the inner self doesn't demand expensive purchases; it only calls for conscious choices. Walk into each room of your home tonight and look at that room in terms of its effect on your inner self. Does walking into the room bring peace and calmness? Do you find you enjoy being in the room, go there often to think and meditate, find delight in the surroundings? Or does the room create havoc in your inner self? Do you want to leave it as soon as you walk through the door? If so, why?

Our surroundings can create either calmness or cacophony. Light streaming through windows brings the calm, healing power of nature into our lives. Often this can be achieved with something as simple as opening a drape or a blind. One dominant color in a room gives harmony to both the surroundings and the inner self.

Achieving this monochromatic calmness may only require some fresh paint. Harmony can also be achieved by simply eliminating those objects whose clashing colors cause discord in the room's decor and in ourselves. Creating calmness and harmony in our environment is a matter of paring down, not purchasing more.

> Our SURROUNDINGS CAN CREATE EITHER CALMNESS OR CACOPHONY

Going through closets, dresser drawers, kitchen cabinets, and files, searching for and eliminating clutter is healing. Try it. You'll be amazed at how much your environment affects your inner self.

Start with clothes closets and dresser drawers. Look at each item and ask, "Have I worn this in the past year? If not, why not? How do I feel when I wear it?" If some piece of clothing keeps getting pushed to the end of the closet or put on the bottom of the pile in the drawer, there is a reason: We don't like it, it doesn't fit, or we don't like who we are when we're wearing it. Give those items to a charity. Next, walk into the kitchen and evaluate each item in your shelves and drawers, asking the same question: "Have I used this in the past year? If not, why not?" Trash or give away every item that is simply taking up shelf space, causing clutter in your environment. Lastly, go to the desk or file cabinet where you keep bills, invoices, coupons, advertisements, and papers, throwing away all ancient paid bills, outdated coupons, and old balanced check statements that will never be needed. The more we practice strengthening the inner self and eliminating "stuff and things," the easier it becomes to simplify, simplify, simplify. We're not *losing* anything; we've *gaining* an environment that encourages inner peace.

Move through each room, asking, "Is this object, this possession, a reflection of me—of the person I'm trying to become? What can I do without? What jars my soul each time I look at it? Get rid of those things—and don't replace them. If one of your life anchors is to be authentic, listen to Thomas Moore when he says, "Surrounded by plastic ferns, we will be filled with plastic thoughts." Habitually making our environment reflect our life anchors opens the door for joy.

Making conscious choices concerning what we're seeing each day is good. Making conscious choices concerning what we're hearing each day is even better.

The music we habitually listen to makes us who we are; which compact discs, audiocassettes, radio stations, and videos we include in our environment will determine who we become. Norman Cousins proved to the world the power of music, doing studies which showed that listening to the lyrics of calming music actually lowered a person's blood pressure and decreased the level of anxiety in her life. In 1845, Longfellow instinctively knew what Cousins later proved in the laboratory: Music heals our body and soul. In his poem "The Day Is Done" he reminds us, "And the night shall be filled with music/And the cares that invest the day/Shall fold their tents like Arabs/And as silently steal away." Enjoying the relaxation and peace that accompanies listening to soothing music, many of us have felt the cares of the day "silently steal away." Keeping in mind what we want the final result of our life to be, we'll carefully choose which music we allow in our environment. By making this habitual, conscious choice, we discover that we control both our environment and our joy.

Make Deposits in Our Mind's Memory Bank

What we habitually put into our memory banks makes us who we are. One of the most powerful habits we'll ever practice is what we stash into the storage bins of our minds. There are two things we humans must do alone: Endure pain and face death. No one can do either for us; no one can be our stand-in. It's going to be just God and us. The internal resources we've cultivated will help us face these circumstances over which we have no control.

> WE'LL DISCOVER WE'LL GET BACK ONLY WHAT WE'VE PREVIOUSLY INVESTED

Our internal resources, however, don't just occur magically in our hour of need; when life collapses around us, we'll discover we'll get back only what we've previously invested. If we've made regular deposits over the years, our memory bank can sustain us through tough times.

What's in our memory banks can occur either by accident or by choice. More often than we're aware, it's by accident. Our minds can, and will, memorize without our even being aware of it. During those rare moments of repose that enter our lives, if we listen to what's playing through the chords of the mind, we may be surprised by what we'll hear.

My friend, who teaches persuasion, has her students take a "pop quiz" in which she gives them popular advertisement slogans, and they write down the name of the product that goes with each slogan. The students are always shocked to discover that they know all the answers, yet they've not consciously memorized any. Repetition is a very effective, sometimes seductive, teacher.

We can, however, commit things to memory by choice. By consciously memorizing poems, prayers, or lyrics that we want in our memory banks, we gain inner strength. When life crumbles all around us, we'll find within ourselves the power and peace we crave.

This current age scoffs at memory. Schools ridicule it; parents say it's outdated. Thank heavens, I was born before memorization became obsolete. I learned early in life that we must feed our minds, just as we feed our bodies. My father taught me that I could make my mind give back to me anything I wanted it to, but only if I'd first made it a part of my memory bank.

Daddy had memorized hundreds of poems and quotations. Being raised in a home where memorizing was not only accepted, but actively practiced, I saw its virtues and watched him reap the results of his labor. Not only did he gain enjoyment in being able to pull entire poems out of his memory and share them with friends; he also found that his memory bank got him through those terrible times when he had to face life alone. I well remember him being pushed back into the cardiac care unit after having had extensive testing and jokingly telling me that he'd probably twisted the tests, giving false readings, because he'd spent the entire time repeating to himself the soothing psalms in his memory bank.

I, too, pull out my comforting quotations when life gets rough. While having an MRI recently, relaxation came easily as I repeatedly let the prayer of St. Francis roll through my mind. Coming out of the MRI tube, I commented to the radiologic technologist, "What do people do who have nothing in their memory bank to pull out?"

Memorizing inspirational and peaceful lines from poetry or scripture has given me the inner strength to get through life's lousy times.

Without making memorization a high priority in our life, needing courage and comfort, we'll likely reach inside our minds and find nothing there but Pepsi jingles and McDonald's commercials.

Our Habitual Comparisons Affect Our Inner Strength

The level of our inner strength is partially determined by our comparisons. And we choose these comparisons. Although it is human to compare our lot in life with that of others, it is wise not to do so, for comparisons always make us either egotistical or envious. Learning to be content with what we have rather than always comparing ourselves to others brings inner strength.

Comparisons with others color our attitudes. Since comparisons have such power, we need an habitual awareness of what and with whom we're comparing ourselves. Unfortunately, we often look around us and find that there's this huge gap between what we have and what we perceive others to have.

Most cities have very affluent, middle-affluent, and less-than-affluent neighborhoods and suburbs. Whenever those of us in the middle drive through the "very," we feel less satisfaction with our own situation than when we drive through the "less-than." For example, when we go to the yearly homearama showcasing mansions costing half a million dollars or more, we return to our own front door feeling we're much worse off than the rest of the world. We may even mope around the house for days, feeling deprived because our home lacks all the neat features we saw in those houses on display. But when we swish through the "less-than" on our way to an elegant restaurant downtown, we're forced to face the fact that we're better off than many. Our earnings, our possessions, and our lives have not changed between these two trips; the only thing that has changed is whom we've chosen to compare ourselves with.

Similarly, many of us compare ourselves only with those colleagues and coworkers who are a step ahead of us, frequently feeling sad because they have larger offices, higher salaries, and more influence with the boss. Seldom do we make the effort to consciously compare our work situations with those who are still struggling to gain what we've already achieved.

Sadly, we often covet what those better off than ourselves possess. But it doesn't have to be that way. Learning to be satisfied with what we have rather than desiring more, more, more—this is the essence of joy. As Seneca says, "No one can be poor that has enough, nor rich, that covets more than he has."

Attitudes become habits; habits determine who we will become. Practicing attitudes and habits that strengthen the soul, we gain inner strength.

You will find as you look back upon your life that the moments that stand out, the moments when you really lived, are the moments when you have done things in a spirit of love.

Henry Drummond, *The Greatest Thing in the World*

⚜ 6 ⚜

MOVE OUTSIDE SELF-CENTEREDNESS

When life is lousy, it's easy to make oneself the center of the universe. Every thought, every action, revolves around "me, me, me." We can extract ourselves from this suffocating self-centeredness by getting tangled up in the joys, sorrows, fears, and frustrations of those around us. Moment by moment, we increase our joy by cultivating the art of connectedness.

As in the 1946 movie *It's a Wonderful Life*, it's the daily contacts we have with those around us that make a difference. Watching the movie, we feel a chord of recognition resonating within us as we ask ourselves: How is my being alive making the world a better place?

Few of us will discover a cure or win a Nobel Peace Prize; few will write a best-seller or be a renowned speaker. Yet all of us will influence, for good or for bad, those people we come in contact with today. As William George Jordan says in *The Majesty of Calmness*, "Man's unconscious influence, the silent subtle radiation of his personality, the effect of his words and acts, the trifles he never considers, is tremendous. Every moment of life is changing to a degree the life of the whole world."

Making this "unconscious influence" the radiation of love, we quit marinating in self-pity. Shaking off our self-centeredness, we reach out to those around us, discovering there are multitudes of people craving connectedness.

The 1990 census showed that nearly one-third of all U.S. households consisted of one person. Although many of these people lead rich and rewarding lives, others feel isolated, unwanted, and unimportant. Not all people who live alone are lonely; not all lonely people live alone. But whether they're alone or in a crowd, anytime they don't feel emotionally connected to a significant person, loneliness becomes an unwanted companion.

Pamela was one of these people. Being divorced for twelve years, she had raised her three children by herself. Struggling through those difficult days of lack of money, late child support payments, and little adult companionship, she'd waited for that joyous day when her three children would be grown. But when the day came, her life echoed with emptiness.

One Saturday my phone rang, and I heard her saying, "Can I come over? I'm having one of those days when I feel terminally alone." "What a wonderful choice of words," I thought.

"Jon left for the service last week. That means no children in the house anymore. It means less food to cook, less clothes to wash, less dishes to do, less bills to pay. I should be elated, ecstatic, having the time of my life, but all I do is cry," she admitted. "This being independent isn't all it's cracked up to be. Since the divorce, I've felt that even though no man needed me, the kids did. It's really rotten to realize that now no one needs me. It makes me wonder why I'm living. I'm not going to get married again at this age. I can't even find a decent person to date, let alone marry. I want the kids to be independent of me, but, darn it, I want someone to need me," she announced. As Pamela talked and I listened, we were connected. Love flowed between us.

Love Has Various Definitions

Love is a powerful life anchor. Yet, many of us shy away from this maligned verb. *Love*, we decide, is an overused, meaningless word. Knowing that 50 percent of marriages end in divorce, we decide that married love is a mirage; realizing we dread holiday reunions, we decide that family love is an illusion. Love, we conclude, is a great concept but an unattainable ideal—an ideal that doesn't work in the real world. Convinced that it would work if only we tried harder, we attempt to "love everybody," only to discover we can't do it. Finding there are people we don't love, people we don't even like, we feel disillusioned.

Discovering the reality that some marriages don't work, the harsh truth that some families don't merge, and the impossibility of loving everyone, too often we throw out the concept rather than admit we may have an unrealistic, perhaps even an inaccurate, definition of love.

Although there are a myriad of definitions that have been given of love, I best like John Powell's. He tells us that the love which brings joy into our lives occurs when we have "concern for the satisfaction, security, and development of the one loved." The love he's describing is a giving love, not a taking one. It goes beyond sexual attraction and shared values. It goes beyond being number one in someone's life, beyond being best friends, beyond feeling close and comfortable.

With this definition, love no longer is a capricious, free-floating emotion; instead, it's a decision to consciously commit ourselves to the joy and well-being of our relatives, friends, and acquaintances. The shape, size, and color of our love for any one person is determined by the level of commitment we've made. Moving outside our self-centeredness becomes easier when we understand:

✦ We Can Love People We Don't Like

✦ Love Is Not Static; It Evolves

Love Promotes the Self-Worth and Joy of Those around Us

Some people have a difficult time dealing with the idea that they can love someone they don't "like." But we can if we've made a commitment, a decision, to do so. Each time we're trying to promote the inner growth and self-worth of another, we're loving her. That doesn't mean we'll necessarily "like" or even "approve" of that person; it simply means we'll try, as best we know how, to promote inner growth and self-worth in her life.

Love means helping that person to be the best person she can be; it means encouraging and applauding. It does not mean judging. Love that has "strings" attached is not love. Love doesn't say, "I'd love you *if* you'd lose weight, save money, do things on time, or

> ◢ LOVE MEANS HELPING THAT PERSON TO BE THE BEST
> PERSON SHE CAN BE; IT MEANS ENCOURAGING AND
> APPLAUDING. IT DOES NOT MEAN JUDGING ◤

learn to listen." No, I can think you weigh too much, spend too much, procrastinate too much, or talk too much—and still try to promote inner growth and self-worth in your life. It may not always be easy, but I can still love you.

Making a commitment to the growth, self-worth, and joy of another person moves me outside myself—outside my self-centeredness and into joy.

Love Takes Us from "I Love You Because . . ." To "I Love You in Spite of . . ."

As love for the significant people in our lives moves from the apple-blossom pink of new love into the rich mahogany of maturity, we replace, "I love you because . . . " with "I love you in spite of . . . ." Realizing that love is not static but always evolving gives us inner strength.

Until we've experienced on a daily basis the rubbing of two souls against each other, we're totally unaware of all the hidden habits each of us possesses. While relationships are still budding and growing, we love someone because—she dresses with style, listens well, has a sense of humor, or likes to play tennis; because—he understands finances, plans wonderful dates, fits in well with our family, or likes to dance. We love him because—he's loyal, hard-working, responsible, or focused. We love her because—she's vivacious, pretty, spontaneous, or emotional.

And then time and reality move our love from newness to maturity. With this movement comes the realization that if we're committed to the growth, self-worth, and joy of that person, we can't love him/her "because" of anything. If he's loyal, hardworking, responsible, or focused—he may also be stubborn, demanding, controlling, or a workaholic; if she's vivacious, pretty, spontaneous, or emotional—she may also be unambitious, clinging, irresponsible, or frivolous.

Although at some gut level we'd like the significant people in our lives to be our own mirror images, they won't. We're individuals, coming into a relationship with our own unique personalities.

One of us is saving, putting a percentage of each paycheck into a mutual fund; the other spends freely and impulsively. One of us is a neatnik, never going to bed until the kitchen sink is clean; the other leaves the Sunday paper strung all over the family room. One of us is organized, filing bills neatly in folders; the other sticks receipts into the most convenient drawer. One of us wears classic, conservative clothes; the other buys each new fad that comes along. One of us wants to talk about feelings; the other wants to talk about facts. One of us brings down balances in the checkbook; the other forgets to fill in the stub. One of us cherishes traditions; the other forgets birthdays and anniversaries.

> ✒ IF WE SHRINK LOVE DOWN INTO A NARROW,
> ONE-COLORED CLOTH, NOT ALLOWING FOR RIBBONS OF
> VARIATION AND RAINBOWS OF COLOR, WE'RE LIMITING ONE OF
> THE MOST POWERFUL FORCES FOR JOY IN OUR LIVES ✒

At some point in every relationship that's going to last, we move from "I love you because . . ." to "I love you in spite of the fact . . . ." At this significant juncture in a relationship, we make a commitment to that person's inner growth, self-worth, and joy. While doing so, we move outside our own narrow self-centeredness, gaining the inner strength we desire.

Love Is a Cloth of Many Colors

There's no way we're going to love everybody with the same intensity or with the same depth. That does not, however, negate the power of love. If we shrink love down into a narrow, one-colored cloth, not allowing for ribbons of variation and rainbows of color, we're limiting one of the most powerful forces for joy in our lives.

Four strong threads weave together to create the cloth of love:

+ Communication
+ Empathy
+ Listening
+ Kindness

Love Grows through Communication and Connectedness

In the past year, which times stand out as being "the best"? Looking back over your entire life, what moments do you remember as the most joyful? Chances are great that you didn't think of the time you redecorated the kitchen, bought the red sports car, or purchased the VCR. You probably didn't even think of being in the National Honor Society, graduating from college, or getting promoted. Although exciting when it occurs, gaining possessions, prestige, or fame is not the stuff of which meaningful memories are made. The moments we remember as being "the best" are nearly always those when we've had conversation and connectedness with another person.

Every day we're making memories. From the moment we get up today until we climb back to bed, each and every conversation we have will become a tiny piece we've placed in the mosaic of our own memory, as well as the memories of everyone whose life touches ours. Today, tomorrow, and every day for the remainder of our lives we're doing much more than living in the present; every day our actions and words become a part of someone's life.

The memories we'll remember will likely be times we felt connected to someone. And this connecting gets done through communication. Because love is a "never-ending conversation," there can't be communication unless people are sharing ideas and feelings. If physical proximity is impossible, writing letters and making phone calls have to replace face-to-face sharing. It's that "being there" that makes love grow. Mortimer Adler in *How to Speak, How to Listen* says, "Human beings cannot form a community or share in a common life without communicating with one another. That is why conversation is the most important form of speaking and listening."

People are hungry for communication and connectedness. Yet, even within our immediate families few hours are spent sharing ideas and feelings. People's schedules are so fragmented that seldom does the entire family spend an hour together in one room. Even that one lone point of communication, the evening meal, is slowly disappearing. Although the current proliferation of individual frozen entrees is marketed to widows, divorcees, and single adults, these entrees are also a subtle symbol of the aloneness that exists within families, people passing in the night, each zapping his own individual entree.

Although we're part of the human community, we also have a longing to be a part of some other community. In the past, home, family, neighborhood, and church have filled this need, but for some these have ceased to be integral parts of modern life. Many of us no longer have extended families living nearby, are not active in a church community, and live in neighborhoods where people lack a sense of closeness and caring.

Having an ongoing but unfulfilled need for communication and connectedness, we hungrily reach for substitutes. And they aren't hard to find. Flipping on the computer is a convenient way to create the illusion that we're experiencing connectedness. As the information highway is bringing us a myriad of possibilities for research and knowledge, it's also bringing the potential for diminishing our humanness as we substitute facts for feelings, leaving us with an incessant hunger for genuine connectedness. While broadening our base of knowledge, giving us access to libraries and people all over the world, it has narrowed the lives of some users. Even as it connects, it isolates.

The exchange of messages in on-line chat rooms can become convenient masks that users hide behind in order to avoid meaningful communication; some users even protect themselves from disclosure with anonymous names. Concealing identity, exchanging facts, playing games, users seldom move beyond facts to feelings. Exchanging information on the Internet is not synonymous with having conversation.

But perhaps more pervasive than the isolation of the on-line services is the isolation brought about by use of the computer itself. If

> EVERY DAY OUR ACTIONS AND WORDS BECOME A PART OF SOMEONE'S LIFE

we live with or are computer users, we're well aware of the addictive quality that this wonderful piece of technology possesses. It's a Pandora's box of experiences and excitement, a never-solved Rubik's Cube, swallowing huge hunks of our time, energy, and attention.

Suddenly we're aware that the computer is absorbing us, taking us away from family, friends, and life. We dash to check E-mail as soon as unlocking the door, rush to see what's on the Internet as soon as dinner is over, spend endless days learning a new software program, and type frantically on our latest project long after the last family member is asleep. And as we become sucked in by the computer's magic, we find ourselves resenting anything that pulls us away from it. All too quickly and easily, we may discover our computers have replaced conversation with family and friends.

Loneliness and Isolation Are Symbols of the Twenty-First Century
An essential element of joy is knowing there's someone who thinks life is more interesting, more exciting, and more wonderful when he's in our presence. You and I want, actually need, to feel that someone's life would be less meaningful if we were dead. We need to know that someone's joy is related to us. Many people, however, don't have this person.

As a result of divorce, death, aging or being single, our world is filled with people who feel: "No one gives a damn if I live or die." Offering them communication and connectedness, we move outside our own self-centeredness.

WHEN DIVORCE ENTERS OUR LIVES, WE FEEL TERMINALLY ALONE Couples divorce and separate, pulling each other and their children in different directions; conversation is often difficult and connectedness impossible.

Recently, Nicki, sitting on my deck and staring into the woods, told me, "This being forty-eight years old, having grown, married children and a husband who no longer wants you is the pits." After Nicki and her husband had raised their children, reality reared its ugly head. When the last child was in college, her husband left her to marry another woman.

Nicki was feeling terminally alone. "I come home at night, walk into that empty house where we lived together for so many years, and the silence is deafening. It's not just a literal lack of noise; it's a lack of life. I'll be brimming over with things that happened at work, things I want to tell someone, and there's no one to tell. I'll be reading a good passage in a book, start to share it with Mike, and remember that Mike's gone. I'm sick of sleeping in an empty bed, tired of eating alone, exhausted from crying. I want someone to scratch my back, open stuck jars, and talk to electricians." She looked at me and asked, "Do I sound childish?" And I answered, "No. You sound human."

WHEN SOMEONE WE LOVE DIES, WE FEEL TERMINALLY ALONE "Does the pain ever get better?" Betsy asked. "Not for a long, long time. It's never over; it never really goes away," I responded. Dealing with the recent death of her husband, Betsy was aching with the agony of aloneness. Since she had no children and her parents were dead, she suddenly found herself feeling totally disconnected from any significant relatives or friends.

As we sat in my living room, she looked at the Christmas wreath hanging over the fireplace and remarked, "I didn't decorate this year. I feel so guilty, but I simply couldn't do it. I hate the holidays." "I know," I replied. "There have been years I've hurt too much to decorate. Don't feel guilty. Only you know what you need."

"I'm not dealing with this at all well," she sobbed. "I've cried so much this week that my stomach hurts. Christmas, every holiday, is just terrible. All I can think about is what we were doing this time last year, what we said, where we went, what we bought. It's like my mind is in past tense. The emptiness of my life is so stark, so real, compared to the pictures that come flashing on the television screen. Everywhere I look I see images of love, togetherness, and connectedness. Holidays are horrible."

Yes, if we've recently experienced a significant loss, holidays are horrible. While advertisements bombard us with pictures of people enjoying one another, we realize we have no one. We recognize that a part of life is gone—over—never to return. We've not only lost a person; we've lost a dream—a dream of what "could have been" and now never can be. During the holidays, we aren't at all sure that living makes much sense.

WHEN AGING ENTERS OUR LIVES, WE FEEL TERMINALLY ALONE Connectedness becomes more difficult to develop as we age. Many older people face seemingly endless days with no significant people left in their lives. Families move and adult children scatter across the United States; death claims our parents. We live longer and find most of our friends and relatives have died. Suddenly, there are no children, no spouse, and few close friends. And replacing those people who used to find joy in our presence becomes more difficult the older we are.

WHEN WE ARE SINGLE, WE OFTEN FEEL TERMINALLY ALONE I meet many single men and women who share this same loneliness and isolation, but hesitate to admit it to the rest of the world—a world which assumes that anyone who has never married must have chosen this situation and therefore be totally content. This, however, is often far from the truth. Although they may have done an excellent job of convincing themselves as well as their friends that their lives are fulfilling, in moments of repose and reflection, they recognize that there are corners of themselves that are empty.

Brittany, a former student and current friend, is one of these people. The world sees her as a successful professional who has achieved the "American dream" of fame, fortune, and prestige. What the world doesn't see are the nights she is alone in her apartment wishing she had someone who cared about what had happened to her that day. Dealing with one of these frustrating evenings, Brittany told me, "Why does everyone refuse to accept the fact that being single is not the bed of roses the women's magazines make it out to be? Sure, it's a life that gives independence and freedom from husband and kids, but independence and freedom bring isolation also. Anymore it is nearly sacrilegious to suggest that a woman would be happier married! But I would. I hate this coming home to an empty apartment and having no one to tell that I closed the biggest deal of my life today. I wish there were someone who would rather be with me than any one else in the whole world." Brittany is not the only single person who feels this way.

Empathetic Loving Radar Is a Thread in the Cloth of Love
Many people have huge pockets of emptiness in their lives. No one can fill the hollow spots within another's soul, but we can give him the strength to fill his own emptiness.

As we reach out to those around us, promoting their growth and self-worth, we're loving them. Doing this successfully means developing what I call "loving radar," staying tuned in to their needs, even while dealing with our own. We begin by simply loving, expecting nothing in return. Slowly we realize that as we reach out to others, we're making their lives more satisfying and increasing our own joy. It's a "win/win" situation.

Attempting to promote the growth and self-worth of those around us, we'll be amazed at the number of people who need our love. And all those people aren't blatantly obvious. Looking at the facade they show the public, we see them handling their lives smoothly and seldom asking for assistance. Yet, most people have moments when they need someone. Just because they've learned to handle life with outward ease doesn't mean they're having an easy time doing it. Using loving radar, we'll sense their need.

If in doubt, ask. Don't make some generic statement such as, "Just call if I can help you sometime." Rather, say, "I'm going to the grocery store this week. Can I get you anything?" "I'm going to the fruit market soon. Can I bring you something?" "I'm going to the mall next week. Do you want to go?" "Let's talk. I'll bring bagels and you fix coffee. What day is good?" Or offer the best statement anyone can receive: "I'm giving you Saturday afternoon. Make a list of the odd jobs you need done around the house." Each week my neighbor Joanne calls to see if I need her to carry the trash to the curb and to ask what she can pick up for me when she's at the grocery store. Her weekly phone calls enrich my life. These direct, specific offers are beautiful presents wrapped in ribbons of love.

Love Is the Answer; It Is in Giving That We Receive
Can we focus our thoughts on giving rather than getting? Can we get outside our self-centeredness when we're feeling so empty, so unneeded?

Feeling alone, we question: "When I'm no longer the most significant person in anyone's life, can I find joy and meaning by loving others? Can I actually live that line in the prayer of St. Francis: 'Grant that I may not so much seek to be consoled, as to console; to be understood, as to understand; to be loved, as to love'?" Time and experience have shown me we can.

Using empathetic loving radar, we reach out to those around us. We start by going to hospitals, nursing homes, and senior citizen centers and saying, "Here I am. Who can I help? What can I do?" We work at a hospice; offer time at a drop-in shelter; serve meals at a homeless shelter; volunteer in an inner city school; read to residents at a nursing home. The opportunities and the needs are endless. By cultivating empathy and losing ourselves in the lives of those around us, we find an inner strength that didn't previously exist. Love that gets us outside our self-centeredness is the answer.

> ◣ AS WE REACH OUT TO THOSE AROUND US, PROMOTING THEIR GROWTH AND SELF-WORTH, WE'RE LOVING THEM ◢

When we crave to be consoled, the best thing we can do is console another; when we ache to be understood, the wise thing to do is to try to understand a hurting friend; when we long to be loved, the most healing thing we can do is to promote the growth and self-worth of those around us. It is in giving that we receive.

Listening Is a Significant Thread in the Cloth of Love

There's a vast difference between hearing and listening. Most people hear; few listen.

Listening is a learned skill; it's not, however, an easy skill. Learning to listen well takes time, effort, and practice. We're not going to make that much effort unless we believe in the power of love. When life is joyless and meaningless, we want someone to know how meaningless it is. More than anything else in the world we want the sense of wonderful relief that comes from realizing that someone knows what it feels like to be us. We want someone to listen.

Lacking Communication with Someone, We Find Substitutes
The two substitutes I use are talking to God and my paper psychiatrist.

Each day I have a running conversation with God, telling him all my fears, frustrations, hopes, and joys. From the moment I get out of bed until I climb back in, I fill each hour with these conversations. Be it mentally or aloud, I'm forever sharing with him my ideas and feelings. When I'm at the end of my string, I tell him; when I'm absolutely elated, I share the news with him. These conversations continue even when I awake in the middle of the night. In fact, some of our best talks are at three A.M. while I'm lying in bed. God helps me realize that he knows what it feels like to be me.

My other substitute is my paper psychiatrist. For many years, my psychiatrist was a manual Remington Rand typewriter; now it's my computer. Over the years, hundreds of pages have been typed, making it possible for me to tell someone exactly what it feels like to be me. Telling my paper psychiatrist each and every emotion rumbling around inside me, I never lie, never hide, never pretend.

At the end of the day, I'll often know life is not right; something's wrong. Having only this vague sense of discontent, I'll not be sure exactly what I'm feeling or why I'm feeling it, but I know something is corrupting my peace of mind. Typing helps me pull my emotions outside myself and place them onto the screen. The longer I type, the clearer my feelings and ideas become. My paper psychiatrist has helped me face, sift through, and deal with the emotional pain that has periodically pounded my life. As typing gives form and focus to my ideas and feelings, I find I'm no longer in the clutches of discontent. Talking to my paper psychiatrist gives me a clear awareness of what it feels like to be me.

We desperately need someone we can talk with on a daily basis, someone who will lovingly listen. Talking to God and typing to a paper psychiatrist are wonderful, healthy substitutes, but they always will remain just that: substitutes.

There are times we need to talk to what my nephew's pastor calls "someone with skin on." That's us. For all the hurting people in the world we can be that person "with skin on." All it takes is our time, our attention, and our love.

Three Ways That Listening Validates People's Feelings
One of the most significant ways we love others is by validating their feelings. We do this when we:

+ Listen to Feelings
+ Listen without Judging
+ Quit Trying to Solve Problems

LISTEN, NOT TO WHAT PEOPLE SAY, BUT TO HOW THEY FEEL Realizing that more often than not people don't say what they really feel, I try to listen between the lines for the feelings the words are masking. Although I often fail, I've found that making the effort, succeeding now and then, makes my own life more rewarding.

Recently when Darlene called to tell me her mother had died, I knew her tears were from more than just the loss of her mother.

"It's been such a long four days," she sobbed. "Everyone is being so kind, bringing in food, stopping to offer sympathy. It seems odd to have all my sisters and brothers back in one house again. Funny, no one has really changed. Angela is still Dad's darling; Cynthia still drinks too much; Tom's still giving orders; and Bill's still unreliable. There are so many relatives that I've cleaned house and done dishes nonstop for four days. But does anyone notice? No. Angela and Cynthia are useless, yet Dad gives them all his attention."

Picking up on the last few sentences, I responded, "You're feeling really unappreciated, aren't you?" That statement opened the door as she told me how isolated, how unloved, she felt. Having everyone together had reminded her of the divisions and differences that had always haunted their family. "I've not only lost Mother; I've lost a family. I'm not important to Dad; I never was, and I never will be. The members of our family have nothing in common; we simply tolerate each other. Now I belong to no one," she replied. We continued talking for an hour as she shared with me all the times in her past when she'd been ignored, neglected, and unappreciated. By my listening between the lines, Darlene had the opportunity to tell someone what it felt like to be her.

Recently I had an opportunity to be on the other end of this conversation; I was the one who longed for someone to listen to what it felt like to be me. No one wanted to.

After nearly forty years of faithfully lifting my paralyzed body in and out of my own car, my shoulder wore out. For the first time since the wreck, I realized I had no choice but to purchase a wheelchair van. And I did. It was the most beautiful kneeling van a person could ask for. It did everything I needed, lowering at a push on a remote control, releasing a ramp for me to enter on, automatically locking my wheelchair in place, and giving me total freedom. And I intensely hated it.

As everyone was crowing with delight, I was seething with anger. I'd experienced one of the most significant losses of my life, but no one wanted to listen. No one saw that even as the van gave me independence, it also took away a great deal, moving me into a new, unwanted phase of life. No one wanted to listen to the fact that I'd lost much more than use of a car. More than ever before, I was trapped by my body. The van symbolized to me a significant passage—a passage I didn't want to occur. With the aging of my shoulder came the aging of my body. Suddenly I was keenly aware that age would slowly take away my coveted independence. And I detested it.

At the same time, however, I was thankful, very appreciative, for the magical machine that would allow me to continue my active life. And, of course, I said so. When people marveled over this new purchase, I'd reply, "Yes, it's been great to be able to easily get places again." And I meant every word. But that didn't diminish my loss, my pain. I wanted someone to know what I was going through, someone to care.

Finally, my nephew's wife, a perceptive person, gave me the opening I needed, asking, "How does it feel to give up your car?" And I told her. Such openings are gifts of love we give each other. You and I have the opportunity, the obligation, to lavishly hand these gifts to all who need them, scattering them with abandon around a world filled with hurting people.

LISTEN TO PEOPLE'S PAIN, EVEN WHEN WE DISAGREE WITH THE CAUSE OF THE PAIN Listening to people even when we disagree with them, we can validate their feelings. Laying my own beliefs and biases aside long enough to put myself in another person's place is a challenge I face daily, a challenge I find demanding and difficult. Teaching college students born in the eighties means being actively involved in the lives of people whose values don't always dovetail neatly with my own.

While they were my students, and later as my friends, many of these people turn to me when life crashes down around them. By lovingly listening, even when I disagree with their actions and attitudes, I can validate their feelings, something each desperately needs. I cannot, however, do this if I allow my own biases and beliefs to block my listening.

The person beside us lacks joy; that lack of joy may have resulted from what we believe were "foolish choices." That in no way negates the fact that the person needs our love. Listening with love does not give a "stamp of approval" to their choices; it simply validates their pain.

When Christy, one of my nursing students, started having an affair with a married doctor at the hospital where she was doing her "clinical," I listened as she went through the roller-coaster ride of emotions that accompanied each weekend together, each weekend apart, each high, each low of their relationship. This continued until she graduated and got a job working on his floor in the hospital. After a year of seductive meetings, secret letters, and silent pain, Christy's affair abruptly came to an end. Telling her he'd

> ◣ LISTENING WITH LOVE DOES NOT GIVE A "STAMP OF
> APPROVAL" TO THEIR CHOICES; IT SIMPLY
> VALIDATES THEIR PAIN ◥

decided to stop the deception, the doctor not only quit sleeping with her; he also saw that she was discharged from the floor where they had both worked.

With the end of both her relationship and her job, Christy fell apart. Phone calls became constant. "Please help. Please listen," she'd say. And I'd reply: "I can't help, but you know I'll listen." By getting her hurt outside herself, by sharing it with me, Christy was able to slowly put the pieces of her life back together again.

Listening to her pain, even when it grew out of actions that I did not agree with, I was able to validate her feelings. It's a gift any of us can give—a gift the world is craving.

LISTEN TO PEOPLE'S DISCOMFORT WITHOUT SLAPPING A SOLUTION ON EVERY PROBLEM   I must constantly remind myself that my responsibility is not to solve people's problems. It's their personal responsibility. I can be someone to bounce ideas off, someone to effectively listen to their thoughts and validate their pain, but I'm not responsible for giving solutions to problems. That's their job.

And yet, how tempting, how tantalizing, to offer a solution for each and every problem.

Former students, current friends, readers, and workshop participants tell me their problems. And often they want advice, solutions, answers. And, to be perfectly honest, often I'd feel much better if I could give them. Listening with love, however, demands that I stifle this very human tendency to take responsibility for someone else's life.

Listening with love means we avoid giving answers and advice. Recently Jason, a recovering alcoholic who had not drunk for over two years, called to tell me that his girlfriend had left him and he saw no reason to go on living, certainly no reason to stay sober. He and I had stayed friends since he was my student, and this was not the first time he'd faced these problems. He wanted answers, solutions, help. As our conversation continued, I sensed how badly he wanted me to solve his problem, how impossible that was, and how trapped I felt because I didn't have answers, solutions, or help. Although every fiber of my being wanted to scream, "This will pass. Don't drink. Please, please don't drink. She'll either come back, or you'll find another girlfriend." I stuffed all those words down inside me, knowing they were not what he needed, or even really wanted. Sure, a magic answer would have been great. Presto! His girlfriend comes back. Presto! He no longer feels life is meaningless. Presto! Alcohol has lost its tempting lure. But joylessness isn't solved by magic.

> ◣ LISTENING WITH LOVE MEANS WE AVOID GIVING ANSWERS AND ADVICE ◤

He and I both knew that he had to feel, work through, and conquer the pain before his life could regain even a smattering of joy. Although I would have felt better by giving him advice, I'd have been doing him a disservice. There were no "answers." Right then all he needed was to share with someone the terrible emptiness that was permeating his soul.

A similar situation occurred last year when Jenny came into my office, sat down, and started crying. Having had her as a student the year before, I knew her husband's death had shattered her world. "It isn't getting any better. I'm just putting in time, trying to get through one meaningless day after another," she lamented. "I have absolutely no one who knows how rotten my life is. People think I'm doing so well. They don't have a ghost of an idea how empty that house is, how often I want to talk to Don, how often I need advice, help, support. I'm sick of being alone, tired of facing every decision by myself. Do you have any idea what it's like to have no one to turn to?" she continued. "Yes," I assured her, "I do. It's really hard."

Jenny continued, "It's just one problem on top of another. And all the little problems build up until I want to scream. Since Don died, I've had to face and deal with all the things that I can't do, never did, and don't even want to learn how to do. I'd never programmed the VCR, replaced the batteries in the clocks, changed the furnace filters, cleaned out the gutters, or figured the taxes. Every time I turn around, I'm facing another problem with no one to help. I miss him so much—his kindness, his warmth. Gosh, I loved him. Losing him is the worst thing that's ever happened to me. But on top of losing him, I've got all these stupid problems facing me."

"I'm tired of living," she announced.

As I listened, I thought how easy it would be to give her "answers and solutions," knowing even as the idea crossed my mind that doing so would be a mistake. There were so many ways I could have "helped" to make her feel better—all ways that would have been unkind. If I'd started suggesting that perhaps she was feeling worse because she was having PMS, I'd have implied that her depression wasn't real, just a reaction to hormones. If I'd started naming people and places she could call to get help with the chores, friends and relatives who could help her learn new skills, I would have been taking away from her the opportunity to let me know what it felt like to be her. And, right now, that was what Jenny needed.

Giving answers slams the door on another person's pain. It's not loving, and it's not effective listening. Someone out there wants us to know what she's going through, wants us to care. This is one of the many times when each of us, the speaker and the listener, just has to hurt. The speaker has to work through her own problems, and the listener has to deal with the discomfort of letting her.

Only with a conscious act of will can we avoid plastering verbal Band-Aids on people's pain. By putting a Band-Aid on a problem, the listener covers it up, encouraging it to fester rather than heal. When talking with someone dealing with the death of a loved one, we sincerely want to make her feel better. Reaching into the medicine cabinet of the mind, we pull out one of the many, much-used verbal Band-Aids that society has placed there. As her tears start flowing, we often mistakenly think it's our job to stop the flow, to ease the pain. It isn't. Our job is to allow the tears to flow, to listen to the pain. Yet, how easily the pat platitudes, "Time heals; you'll feel better in a few months," and "All things are for the best; there's a reason we just don't understand," can come slipping off our tongue and out our mouths.

Part of us wants to make the person feel better, but a lot of the motivation behind our words is to make US feel better. We're extremely uncomfortable when faced with all the unknown and unresolved aspects of grief, and to ease some of that discomfort, we grab these platitudes. Rather than comfort and console the person, we're inadvertently and unthinkingly pushing her pain and sorrow deeper inside, postponing and hindering her healing.

Slapping solutions on a person's problem does not validate her pain.

We can be an effective listener if we're willing to move outside our own self-centeredness and make room in our lives for the feelings of another. As we listen not only to the words but, more importantly, to the emotions; put our own beliefs and biases aside long enough to put ourselves in another's place; stifle the very human desire to give easy answers and soothing solutions—we'll be listening with love.

Politeness, Good Manners, and Kindness Are Threads of Love

Anytime we look at life through the eyes of another person, anytime we change our actions or attitudes to make her life more pleasant, we're showing love. We do this by being polite, using good manners, and showing kindness. Doing this repeatedly we gain inner strength.

Near the end of the nineteenth century, Henry Drummond, in *The Greatest Thing in the World*, defined *politeness* as "love in trifles" and *courtesy* as "love in little things." He believed that the "one secret of politeness is to love." Rearing me in the middle of the twentieth century, my mother reflected his beliefs. She repeatedly reminded me, "Think how the other person feels. If you put yourself in his place and try to feel what he's feeling, you'll always be polite." Any time we follow her advice, we're showing love. And the opportunities for doing so are endless.

Thank-You Notes Are Acts of Politeness, Good Manners, and Kindness

Following my mother's example, I found that manners and politeness came naturally. Thank-you notes were no longer something I "had" to write. After picking out presents for people I loved, I knew how exciting it was to discover they liked my carefully chosen gift; I waited with anticipation for the smile, the recognition, that I'd chosen well. Knowing how good I felt receiving that recognition, it was easy to realize that others felt the same way. If the person wasn't in the same room with me when I unwrapped his gift, I wanted to let him know how much I appreciated his thoughtfulness. Mother showed me that good manners and politeness are inherent parts of love.

Phone Conversations Can Be Acts of Politeness, Good Manners, and Kindness

Before beginning a phone conversation, it would be kind to tell the listener who we are and ask if it's a convenient time to talk. Unless we speak with someone nearly every day, it's not easy to recognize a person's voice, yet we sometimes jump into a conversation, leaving our listener playing "Twenty Questions," trying desperately to identify who we are. Asking if it's a convenient time to talk gives the person an opening to tell us if it's not; all telephone calls are interruptions, but some are terribly inconvenient. Kindness demands we allow the person on the other end of the line to tell us if that is the case.

> KINDNESS AND GOOD MANNERS ARE CAUGHT MORE EASILY THAN THEY'RE TAUGHT

Another time we can show kindness on the phone occurs when we dial a wrong number. We do this by letting the person know it's our fault his phone rang. When we hang up rather than respond, we're being selfish, often leaving the person holding the phone fearful and frightened. Saying "I'm sorry. I dialed the wrong number," we can easily wipe away hours of worry for the person we mistakenly dialed.

And perhaps the nicest and easiest way to be kind on the telephone is to talk slowly and distinctly when leaving a message on an answering machine. If we look at life through the eyes of the person who is going to replay that message, we'll slow down. We've all had the experience of playing and replaying a message, trying unsuccessfully to distinguish the name and the phone number of the caller.

Daily Conversations Can Be Acts of Politeness, Good Manners, and Kindness

Our casual conversations create the persons we are becoming. At workshops, I often ask people to make a list of all the people they talked with that day. Making the list creates an awareness that most of us talk with many people during any given day. Then I suggest that we can increase the joy in our lives, as well as in that of others, if we try for the next twenty-four hours to be pleasant to every person we meet. It's an interesting exercise—an exercise that, with practice, can become an integral part of our daily lives. Talking with the secretary in our office, the teller at the bank, the custodian in our building, the man repairing our washer, the clerk at the discount store, the waitress at the restaurant, the attendant at the hotel, or the bus driver—give us opportunities to make life more pleasant for those around us. All make the threads of kindness stronger in our own lives.

Our attitudes and actions during these casual conversations cut the grooves of our personality, giving us either a meaningful life or a joyless existence.

Kindness, good manners, and politeness are threads of the cloth we call love. Even though we find it very difficult to love every person we come in contact with each day, we certainly can be kind and polite. Often, however, we aren't.

Kindness and good manners are caught more easily than they're taught. Because these are two important strands in the fabric of love, the younger generation needs to see adults practicing both. Yet, the message being sent to society through many television commercials, as well as some programs, is that kindness and politeness are for nerds. The images filling our family rooms neither practice nor applaud politeness or good manners. Adults, usually parents or teachers, are often portrayed as stupid idiots whom the younger generation back-talks, bad-mouths, and ridicules.

In many advertisements, kindness and politeness are mocked. For example, Chester's Pizza showed two local radio personalities arguing and fighting over a pizza; Skyline Chili had a mother and daughter whining and complaining about a truck parked in the driveway; Arby's ran a commercial showing children breaking into a piggy bank and stealing money to buy a sandwich; Drug Emporium portrayed a negative, screaming, witchlike mother making her children buy school supplies; Tyson Chicken introduced a family visiting Aunt Ellen, making fun of her cooking, whispering rude comments, and acting with total disrespect; All Sport had an adult making sensible statements while the picture imposed on the sound was of teenagers mocking the statements being made. These advertisements, and others like them, weaken the threads of love in our lives.

As we cultivate the art of conversation and connectedness and develop loving radar toward those around us, we're able to crawl outside our self-centeredness. Finding people we can help, giving them our time and attention, listening effectively to those who need us, and practicing kindness every day of our lives, we become more loving—and walk toward joy. This joy occurs as we realize that the threads of love create one of our strongest inner resources. They produce a rock-solid inner strength that stays with us in the midst of trials and turmoil.

Let us say what we feel, and feel what we say;
let speech harmonize with life.

Seneca

⚓ 7 ⚓

ALLOW OURSELVES TO BE AUTHENTIC

I n order to promote the inner growth and self-worth of those around us, in order to effectively listen, encourage, and applaud them, we need to be authentic, giving them our most genuine self, not some carefully constructed facade.

Profile of an Authentic Person

Authentic people are more autonomous, more able to "go against the crowd." They can more easily question authority; more easily write their own life script, rather than blindly follow their parents' or their peers' scripts. Likewise, they also have less need to mindlessly rebel, have less trouble agreeing with the values of authorities, parents, or peers when those values are congruent with their own life anchors. Authentic people know their "bottom line" and live in harmony with it.

Being authentic means scrutinizing our beliefs and choices, holding them up to the prism of the core self, questioning and asking, "Is this belief or choice harmonious with my life anchors? Is it helping me become the person I want to be? Is it making my world, as well as the world of those around me, a better place? Is it life-affirming? Is it loving?"

It's all too easy to stifle our authenticity; in fact, society encourages us to do so. You and I, however, know when we're doing this, know when we're going against our best self. Whenever we find ourselves having mindless, meaningless conversations with people whose values we dislike; attending parties and functions we hate; failing to follow our life passion; indiscriminately obeying rules or conventions; neglecting to speak up for our values in committee meetings—then we know we're not being authentic.

At some level, authenticity, as well as the inner strength it generates, is almost always the result of struggle and hardship. Sad, but true, those of us who can easily allow ourselves to be authentic usually have come through our own private, personal hell. And we've managed to do this by allowing ourselves to fully feel the rage, grief, loneliness, fear, hurt, or humiliation that was surging through our souls at that time. We've known the depths of despair, walked through them and, as a result, now have a clearer sense of who we are and what's important.

But we all know people who have gone through the depths of despair, yet won't allow themselves to be genuine, won't allow themselves to be authentic. As a result of some rotten reality that occurred earlier in their lives, they now face each day with frozen emotions. Fearing to face the pain throbbing through their inner selves, these people remain mired in joylessness.

Being authentic means being true to our life anchors—being true to our soul. We allow ourselves to cultivate this authenticity when we:

+ Thaw Our Frozen Feelings
+ Say No to Some Activities
+ Say No to Some Environments
+ Say No to Some People
+ Tear Down Our Masks and Facades

Frozen Feelings Can Be Thawed

Although craving genuine joy, many people are either incapable or unwilling to thaw those emotions that childhood environment or adult circumstances froze. It doesn't have to be that way if we:

+ Admit Our Feelings to Ourselves
+ Share Those Feelings with a Chosen Few

First Thawing Step: Admit to Ourselves How We Feel

Admitting our feelings sounds so easy; it seems so simple. It's not. On the contrary, admitting our feelings is frightening.

We avoid this first step by telling ourselves that if we probe the pain we've so carefully anesthetized, perhaps those feelings will overwhelm us, leaving us more joyless than we are now. After all, we reassure ourselves, now we've at least got a protective facade, a carefully constructed mask that keeps us safe. Why tear it down?

> **◢ MANY PEOPLE ARE EITHER INCAPABLE OR UNWILLING TO THAW THOSE EMOTIONS THAT CHILDHOOD ENVIRONMENT OR ADULT CIRCUMSTANCES FROZE ◤**

Why go inside and disturb the carefully blanketed, neatly laid-to-rest emotions that we have no desire to feel?

Why? Because frozen feelings slam the door on authenticity; opening that door, allowing ourselves to be authentic, brings marvelous inner strength.

There's a paradox here: The very act of admitting we have a powerful, negative feeling gives us control over it. We master the emotion rather than having the emotion master us. It requires patience, self-love, and courage to coax drugged feelings out in the open, to admit to ourselves how much we've been hurt. But this trip inside ourselves is worth all the courage, love, and patience we can give it.

We begin by simply verbalizing to ourselves how we're feeling. Writing these feelings on paper gives them life, makes them real. If we have a typewriter or computer, this step is going to be a lot easier and faster, but pencil and paper still work well. Think about what feeling would be throbbing through you if you'd only let it surface. Sit quietly and feel. Is it fear? Anger? Joy? Rejection? Loneliness? Love? Humiliation? Hurt? Writing about our feelings helps thaw them. If we're afraid, frustrated, fearful; if we're filled with rage, rejection, or regret; if we're feeling unloved, unappreciated, and unwanted; if we're wildly happy, deeply appreciative, madly loving—we need to verbalize to ourselves how we're feeling. In those moments of reflection and repose, we'll get acquainted with those parts of our inner selves that we fear facing.

We create wholeness as we develop this authentic relationship with the inner self. When this occurs, we no longer have to deny a section of our being; no longer is there a constant inner struggle going on. Headaches become fewer, upset stomachs appear less, racing heartbeats grow calmer, muscles relax, skin rashes fade, back pain diminishes. Our body and soul are no longer waging a constant war. We now become free to be the persons we really want to be.

Second Thawing Step: Share Our Feelings with a Chosen Few
Developing an authentic relationship with our inner self brings partial joy; sharing that inner self with a carefully selected friend makes whole what was only partial.

Verbalizing our feelings gives them validity. Thawing frozen feelings that have profoundly affected us in the past means not only knowing what they are, but sharing them with one trusted friend. Having a clinical psychologist or a valued friend lovingly listen to the feelings that have been scrunched down inside us for so long is healing. Without this sharing, we'll be limiting the level of joy in our lives.

If we're very fortunate we'll have one close confidante with whom we can be *totally* authentic; if we're blessed beyond belief, we'll have two. More than that is probably impossible. Although we can't be *totally* authentic with the majority of people we come in contact with, we'll soon discover that the higher the level of authenticity we can have with people, the more meaningful our life will be.

Maintaining this authenticity often means emotionally detaching ourselves from activities, people, and environments that cut long, deep scratches into the soul, marring the integrity we're attempting to maintain. Saying no to toxic activities, environments, and people means saying yes to our best selves.

To be genuinely authentic, we need to become lovingly independent, trusting our life anchors and our inner selves. I use the phrase, "lovingly independent," for we're going to need to believe in ourselves before we can take those tiny beginning steps toward authenticity.

Allowing ourselves to be authentic, we'll find that some activities, environments, and people strengthen us, while others cause cracks and fissures in our inner core. This discontinuity ruptures our authenticity and leaves us joyless. The more firmly we're knotted to this life anchor, the easier it's going to be to say no to anything that would weaken or harm it.

We Gain Integrity When We Learn to Say No to Some Activities

At the end of each day you and I need to think back over the last twenty-four hours and ask ourselves if that time was spent in activities that were congruent with our life anchors. Did those activities strengthen our relationship with ourselves, with others, and with our God? Did they strengthen the core self? I've found that unless I take responsibility for saying no to some activities, I easily trap myself into a "poor me; I've got so much to do" mode. I look at my to-do list and panic.

In both my professional and personal life, I've always had trouble saying no to activities, even those that are not in harmony with the person I'm trying to become.

Professionally, my biggest hurdle is committee meetings. When I was a new, inexperienced teacher jumping the required academic hurdles, I had no choice; I had to serve on committees. In the academic world, committee work is as important for promotions as good teaching is. But now, serving on committees is my choice. Although serving on them certainly strengthens my chances for merit pay and praise from my colleagues, if I allow myself to be authentic, I must ask if those hours I'm spending in meetings are really enriching my core self. And since I've never met an academic committee that helped me become the person I want to be, I choose not to serve. I'll relinquish merit pay for inner peace.

Personally, my nemesis was being available night and day for anyone who "needed" me. When I was younger, I thought if I didn't give that workshop, go to that party, be on that radio talk show, I might miss a chance to give someone a reason to go on living, might miss an opportunity to encourage a hurting person. At some subconscious level, I thought I was responsible for erasing the world's joylessness. Obviously, I thought I was living in harmony with my life anchors. I wasn't.

> ◣ I'VE LEARNED THAT SAYING NO TO AN ACTIVITY THAT FAILS TO HELP ME LOVE EITHER MYSELF, OTHERS, OR LIFE MEANS SAYING YES TO MY CORE VALUES ◢

In the process of overextending myself, I depleted, rather than strengthened, my inner resources. Trying to be all things to all people (an impossible and ridiculous task), I nearly sabotaged my joy. Gaining self-awareness and allowing myself to be authentic, I finally realized what I was doing.

This awareness lessened the guilt that had previously come from saying no. And with this awareness came inner peace. Lots of people still "need" me, but my helping is now given in harmony with my own rhythm, my own pace, and my own needs. Knowing I can't give when I'm depleted myself, I periodically and purposefully rest, relax, and regroup.

Taking a deep breath, I look at each item on my to-do list, each invitation to socialize, each request to talk, and start slashing. I can slice through the trivial trash that is junking up my life by asking, "Is this activity going to help me become the person I want to be? Will it strengthen those qualities I feel are important?" If it won't, it probably deserves, and usually gets, a no.

I've learned that saying no to an activity that fails to help me love either myself, others, or life means saying yes to my core values.

We Gain Integrity When We Learn to Say No to Some Environments

One of the few joys of aging is finally feeling that we're beginning to know what we stand for and who we are. Although we're never "made," but always "becoming," time and experience help us to hear with crystal clarity that still small voice inside us, that voice which persistently pulls us back to what's important in life.

A great deal of the joy in my life comes from saying no to environments that are not in harmony with my core self, that won't help me become the person I want to become. Because I've found that nature, solitude, and books create an environment that enriches my soul, the radio, TV, VCR, and air conditioner are seldom turned on in my home, not because I think they are bad in and of themselves, but because they invade what is important to me. I choose not to stay in a sterile air-conditioned house when by simply opening the windows, I can smell the outdoors, hear the birds and insects, and feel the breeze. The sound, smell, and feel of nature resonates a pleasing, deep inner chord within me. I choose not to have the noise from the TV, radio, or VCR when my own thoughts and the thoughts I get from books bring the insights, inspiration, and motivation needed for me to live in harmony with my life anchors.

Yesterday, I was aware once again how saying no to some elements of my environment means saying yes to my core self. While working on a manuscript, I become immersed in it. All my thoughts, all my actions, all my inner conversations revolve around whatever it is I'm writing. And I've discovered that the most fertile time for incubation is in the hours after I awake. It's a special time when thoughts that have germinated from yesterday, thoughts that were cultivated and rearranged during the night, slowly start to emerge. Although I usually turn on the radio for a half hour each morning, so I'll know what's going on in the rest of the world, I've not done that this week. Doing so would not be authentic, would disrupt my train of thought, would allow some outside person to shatter my focus. It would mean taking away the solitude I crave, allowing someone to cut the threads of thought that are slowly, silently weaving themselves into ideas.

Saying this no means going against the stream of modern life. For a long time I felt guilty because I wasn't fitting into society's lifestyle, wasn't in harmony with its value system, and I'd try to justify, to rationalize, my choice of environment. But over time, I've learned to feel more comfortable with who I am and what I'm living for. Tolerance and love demand that I let others have their lifestyles, their value systems; authenticity demands that I quit trying to justify my own. It's my life—my journey, my joy.

We Gain Integrity When We Learn to Say No to Some People

As we become more authentic, we'll emotionally detach ourselves from people who keep us from living in harmony with our integrity.

In order to be joyful, at some point in our lives we'll want to become emotionally independent of our past. That's going to mean thoughtfully questioning our present attitudes, actions, choices, and beliefs. We're cleaning out the attic of the inner self, saving the precious and discarding what no longer fits. Being independent does not mean tearing ourselves away from our past; it means gluing ourselves to those parts of our childhood that are congruent with what we want to become and separating ourselves from those that aren't.

As we thaw our frozen emotions, as we allow ourselves to become more authentic, we'll become keenly tuned-in to who bolsters our inner growth and who retards it. We'll not only know with whom we can be authentic; we'll also know at what level authenticity is possible with that person. If we must tiptoe on a verbal tightrope when in someone's presence, we're not being authentic. If we're emotionally drained when that person walks out the door, we've not been authentic.

> ◣ WHEN TWO PEOPLE MEET WHO HAVE A CLEAR SENSE OF SELF AND ARE AUTHENTIC, BEAUTIFUL FIREWORKS FOLLOW ◢

The more authentic we're able to be with a person, the more we'll love him. The less authentic we're able to be, the more we'll want to emotionally disengage from that person.

Emotional disengagement is not severance. It might be, but it need not be. Let's say that the person we can't be authentic with is our spouse, brother, or mother. Does that mean we'll sever relationships with that relative? Maybe. Maybe not. If we've come through incest; if we've experienced child abuse; if we've been physically beaten by our spouse—we may choose severance.

Many of us, however, have a host of other reasons why we can't be authentic when we're with a particular person. And for us, severance may not be the answer. Severance eliminates short-term pain, but doesn't always generate long-term gain. It's always easier to "cut and run"; it's not always best. Severance means we are all frozen in time, something I choose not to believe. Severance means we're not going to change, nor is the other person. A healthy substitute for severance is distance, both distance of space and distance of time. Each of us must choose his own limits. And those limits will vary depending on the reasons authenticity is difficult with that particular person.

If we don't enjoy being around someone, that may very well have nothing to do with authenticity. Disagreeing on surface, shallow, insignificant likes and dislikes simply shows we're not cookie-cutter replicas of each other. Thank heavens! With these people, we look for and enjoy their positive qualities, ignoring as much as possible those trivial traits we wish they didn't possess.

Being authentic goes much deeper than this. It is feeling secure with the person we want to be, knowing what we stand for, knowing what we value, knowing what's important, and protecting our inner self from activities, environments, or people who would damage it. It is not lashing out at all who disagree with us; it is not hurting other people's feelings. It is being able to give the best of me to the best of you.

When I give you my positive, authentic self, I touch your inner core, making a joyful difference in your life. I am loving you.

Before entering any new or awkward situation, I often tell myself, "Just be authentic. Be genuine." Any time our personality merges and meets another, we're going to create some sparks, some friction. Friction can be either positive or negative. Relationships can either create magnificent fireworks, bringing beauty into our lives, or malevolent bonfires, bringing destruction and devastation. When two people meet who have a clear sense of self and are authentic, beautiful fireworks follow.

Being authentic helps me touch the inner core of those around me.

We Gain Integrity As We Tear Down Our Masks and Facades

Giving those around us authenticity often means facing fragments of ourselves that we'd just as soon keep hidden. Being authentic sometimes means tearing down the masks and facades society encourages and applauds. We do this as we:

+ Start Listening to Our Tears

+ Stop Hiding behind Roles

Tears Help Us Find the Authentic Self

Beth experienced the pain of tearing down her mask each time she allowed herself to cry. After being married for twenty-one years, her husband asked for a divorce and married another woman. Facing life alone and dealing daily with the pain of rejection, she often called to talk. A few days ago the phone rang, and I heard Beth crying.

"I've been fighting tears all day, but until only a few moments ago I'd been keeping them under control," she sobbed. "I was listening to the radio and doing decently until "You Light Up My Life" came on. That was "our song"! Every single word brought back the life that is no longer mine. I don't "light up his life" anymore; she does. And then I lost it. I totally lost it. I cried until I was exhausted, cried until no more tears would come."

"I lost it." We always say that when we cry. If we've been fighting and holding our tears inside us and then some outside situation becomes the "final straw" and makes us cry, we say, "Oh, I lost it. I just totally lost it."

Really, the more appropriate phrase might be, "I found it." For the moment the tears start to flow is the moment we come face-to-face with our feelings. For those few moments we get in touch with our real selves and our honest emotions.

Over time, I've learned to listen to my tears. Always, without fail, they are telling me something about myself I've been trying to ignore. It's usually some painful feeling that I've crunched up into a tight little wad and stuffed inside myself. That festering, fermenting feeling finally comes to the surface. I experienced this recently while shopping at Kenwood Towne Center. As I passed an older man wearing glasses, smoking a pipe, walking briskly with coattails flying behind him, the tears started sliding down my face. Emotionally, I'd just passed my father. Shaking with tears, I longed for the man who had flown around the Muncie mall in similar fashion. My pain at that moment was as intense as the day I buried him. And I let myself grieve once again.

I had a similar experience of listening to my tears last spring when I was flipping through the pages of the Sunday paper and saw pictures taken of students at a local prom. Looking at one of the girls dressed in a strapless evening gown, I felt the tears start to flow. Soon I was sobbing uncontrollably, aching for the Barbara who had worn a similar gown, danced effortlessly, and felt beautiful. And I let myself grieve for the losses that paralysis had handed me—for losses that could never completely be erased.

In a society that feels uncomfortable with genuine emotions, allowing ourselves to feel and express our pain is difficult. Doing so, however, is the key to inner strength. I was reminded of this truth after the tornado that ravaged our neighborhood. As demolition

> ◣ OVER TIME, I'VE LEARNED TO LISTEN TO MY TEARS.
> ALWAYS, WITHOUT FAIL, THEY ARE TELLING ME SOMETHING
> ABOUT MYSELF I'VE BEEN TRYING TO IGNORE ◢

crews clawed up and tore down the remaining skeletons of over twenty houses, I knew they were destroying much more than buildings. They were chewing up people's lives, memories, dreams, and stability. And I vicariously experienced their pain. Amazingly my one-story ranch suffered the least damage of any house, and as my neighbors were tearing their homes down, contractors were rebuilding my own. Logic said I should be thankful, even elated that my home was being rebuilt. But I wasn't elated. I felt as if I'd experienced a death. And I had. However, few people understood. Repeatedly I was told, "You're one of the lucky ones. You didn't lose your family, your belongings, or your house." It was true. I was back in my rebuilt home, while all my neighbors were still living in hotels and apartments. I had every reason to be "happy, content, and overjoyed." But I wasn't. Rather, I was fighting tears each and every day.

Realizing I had to find the reason for this overwhelming grief, each time the tears would start to surface, I forced myself to stop, listen, and feel. Digging beyond the immediate pain, searching for the cause of that pain, I realized that I was grieving for the loss of youth, the loss of a second chance, the loss of hopes. I was going through a huge passage of life, one that would forever mark the end of what was and the beginning of what now would be. I was experiencing the loss of twenty-four years of planning, planting, and nurturing a wooded sanctuary—a sanctuary that could not be replaced in my lifetime. My healing began when I started being authentic with myself, listening to my tears, and facing hidden fragments within myself.

Rather than tightly crunching our tears down inside ourselves, we'd be wise to "lose control" and find our genuine pain, our authentic agony. By facing and feeling the pain and agony, we release ourselves from bondage. At that moment when the tears flow, we find ourselves; we don't "lose" anything.

Authenticity Allows Us to Quit Hiding behind Roles

Taking the journey inward gives us a clear sense of self—a sense of self that allows us to be genuine and authentic. We know who we are, separate and distinct from any roles, jobs, or professions we have; we're well aware that roles, jobs, and professions are not us. We know we're more than a wife, mother, husband, father, secretary, lawyer, teacher, or carpenter. We know we're more than the R.N., D.D.S., M.D., C.P.A., or Ph.D. that goes after our name.

It's so easy to hide behind our roles. I try, although I sometimes fail, to give my students my most authentic self. Before entering the classroom, I'll think, "Just be authentic; be genuine. Give them the most positive, loving Barbara you can give." And it works. I don't "act a part" or "play a role." What they see is what they get. My hopes, joys, fears, and frustrations concerning our class are openly shared with them. If I make a mistake, handle a situation poorly, or hurt a student's feelings, I admit my error, correct the situation, and apologize.

I'm human. I blow it sometimes. But I try, really try, to let the students know I'm sorry.

I well remember an incident that occurred at Ball State University during my fourth year of teaching. New, unsure, and still learning to handle "off-the-wall" responses, I reacted with criticism to a student's comment. Knowing I'd spoken out of frustration and lack of experience, knowing I'd responded as Barbara would not have responded in any other situation, the next morning I waited outside the classroom and apologized, honestly telling the student why I'd acted as I did. After that, his attitude toward class became more positive, and mine toward him more open and accepting.

Each of us is either genuine, or fake; we're either in touch with the essence of our inner selves, or pretending, hiding behind symbols, images, and masks. Getting in touch with the authentic person inside ourselves, we're able to drop and ignore the masks and symbols many of us hide behind.

Inner strength comes from knowing who we are and who we want to become. Knowing this, our number-one job in life is to become that person. We do this by getting in touch with our authentic inner self, and then working to easily present that authentic self to the rest of the world.

Life is not lost by dying.
Life is lost minute by minute, day by dragging day,
in all the thousand uncaring ways.

Stephen Vincent Benet

LIVE LIFE IN THE NOW

Time is the stuff of which life is made. Yet, how often we unthinkingly squander it. We say we're "killing time," but no one kills only time. He kills life. And many of us are committing suicide daily.

We gain inner strength by cultivating a conscious awareness of the current moment. Because our lives consist of present moments—right here, right now—joy is created as we develop attentiveness to what is going on both inside and outside ourselves each and every moment of our lives. I like to call this living in the Now.

Attentiveness to the Present Gives Inner Strength

Minutes become hours, hours slide into days, and these days slowly, silently slip together, creating a lifetime. A practiced attentiveness to how we're spending our present moments brings joy; "killing time" becomes a diversion, a detour, not the major highway of our life. If we're serious about cultivating inner strength, we're going to be serious about living in the Now. How we spend today, this very hour, determines if we enrich or bankrupt our inner self.

We can choose to mindfully live in the Now, or we can mindlessly sleepwalk through life, totally oblivious to what is going on. Developing this attentiveness to the present is a learned skill, a skill that anyone can possess with practice. Yet, looking around us we find that few people make the effort.

This total oblivion of the Now can often be seen when watching people in a restaurant. More often than not, they'll be eating in a hurried, mechanical manner, as if it's something that has to be done, not something to be enjoyed. Although nutritionists encourage us to eat slowly, savor the colors and textures of the food, notice the atmosphere and the setting, and talk of pleasant subjects, many people are content to gulp the food, ignore the atmosphere, and eat in silence.

Recently while a friend and I were eating at one of Cincinnati's riverfront restaurants, we saw an example of this. In this pleasant setting, the Ohio River puts on a private show for all diners. During the time we were there, we got to see over thirty boats, four barges, a hot-air balloon, and an ultralight plane. And in the background was the always breathtaking Cincinnati skyline silhouetted against an azure sky. To top it off, while we were eating, the Mississippi Queen glided by in all her grandeur.

The couple next to us, however, might just as well have been sitting in their kitchen as they blindly went through the motions of eating, oblivious to everything around them. They came in after we did, talked little, ignored the changing scene, ate automatically, and left a half hour before we did. Awareness didn't seem to be a part of their lifestyle. Unfortunately, the same can be said for a lot of the rest of us.

Attentiveness is part of my lifestyle only because I work at it. Making living in the Now an integral part of each day takes effort, especially for people like me who have a need to be in control. Only by allowing myself to quit trying to control each and every moment can I slow down, sit still, and invite attentiveness into my life.

> ATTENTIVENESS IS A LIFE ANCHOR THAT ENRICHES THE SOUL—AND IT'S OURS FOR THE ASKING

Living in the Now means consciously being aware of what is going on around us. Today I've been writing outside, allowing myself to absorb the beauty of my backyard. Periodically, I take breaks in order to listen to the sounds, inhale the air, and view the scene. I'm putting aside my passion for control in order to practice the "fine art of doing nothing." I quit planning, preparing, working, controlling—and simply AM: I'm aware of the wonderful feel of the warm sun on my bare arms, the breeze gently blowing across my face, the cold glass of iced tea in my hand; the smell of the neighbor's just-cut grass; the sight of the princess spirea throwing a splash of pink across the yard, silhouetted by the woods behind it. I'm aware of the turtle slowly creeping across the patio, the two ducks taking a nap under my copper beech tree, the chipmunk scurrying from his burrow to the woods, and the goldfinches making yellow streaks across the indigo sky. These sounds, sights, and smells enrich my life.

But this attentiveness didn't occur automatically; I had to make it happen. Whether or not I become aware of this soul-enriching day is my choice. I could easily sit on this same deck in this same yard and mindlessly keep writing this chapter, or type letters, or pay bills, or grade essay tests, totally oblivious to the wonder around me. By deliberate choice, I'm not. Rather, I'm choosing to mindfully experience the present moment.

Attentiveness is a life anchor that enriches the soul—and it's ours for the asking.

This attentiveness to what is going on within and around us occurs when we:

+ Know Our Vocation Is Not Our Job
+ Develop a Passion for Paid and Unpaid Activities
+ Cut Life Up into Small Slices
+ Become a Rainbow Sprinkler

Make a Distinction between Our Job and Our Vocation

"What's your job?" "What do you do for a living?" "What field are you in?" "Where do you work?" All these questions really mean: "What do you do so you can pay the bills?" Although we usually refer to this as our "vocation," it's more accurately our "job." In contrast, our vocation is living in harmony with our life anchors.

Our job is what we do for a living; our vocation is why we're living. Our vocation is to live well, not to earn a living; living well is something we can do at any moment of any day. Making a distinction between what we do to make a living and what we do to enrich our life makes us keenly aware that our vocation is not our job. By staying tuned in to those around us, we may, even in the midst of a relatively unexciting, ordinary job, find ourselves actively practicing our real vocation, strengthening our life anchors. Of course, some jobs bring more opportunities for this than others, but opportunities will develop in all jobs if we're looking for them.

Let's face it. Some of our jobs are repetitious, unsatisfying, and boring. But jobs are necessary. They help us support ourselves and our families. The skills, talents, or professions that pay the bills may or may not bring us joy, but how we act while we're at that job can.

Because I'm a professor, society may think I have more of these opportunities to exercise my real vocation than others do. I can assure you from firsthand experience, however, that these meaningful moments don't usually happen when I'm behind the desk. On the contrary, they occur outside the classroom—in the hall, in the office, at my home, or on the phone. They often don't even happen the same quarter that I'm a student's teacher; rather, they develop months, even years, later. These incidents occur when I'm attempting to live in harmony with my personal life anchors.

We have the opportunity to practice our *real* vocation no matter where we are. For example, I can attempt to be tenacious, positive, loving, authentic, and attentive at any moment of any day—whether I'm in the classroom and getting paid, or after I've left the classroom and I'm not getting paid.

If we have a passion for an activity, it absorbs us, pulling us like a magnet, becoming an insatiable desire for more. Developing this passion for both our paid and unpaid activities helps us live in the Now.

Blessed are those of us who get paid for doing something we enjoy, something we have a passion for. I'm one of those fortunate people. Although I have absolutely no desire to retire, I know that inevitable day is approaching. Were I to win a twenty-million-dollar lottery today, I'd likely continue teaching. I realize I'm in an enviable position, one not shared by all my colleagues. I love what I do, and the miracle is that I get paid for doing it. Teaching gives me opportunities to live in harmony with my life anchors; the paycheck is needed, but secondary.

I'd really not consciously thought about how much I enjoy teaching until a few months ago, when our university did a survey of all teachers nearing retirement age, in an attempt to discover what incentives it could offer to make us retire early. When the phone rang and I discovered the purpose of the survey, I tried to answer honestly all the questions I was asked. Patiently I responded to each incentive on the list. "Would you take early retirement if . . . ?" Repeatedly, I answered, "No." Feeling sorry for the poor man on the other end of the phone who had spent nearly five minutes listening to my nos, I finally explained, "Nothing would make me take early retirement. What I get from teaching is not measurable in money; I teach because I love it." There was a pause on the other end of the line, and finally he replied, "You're really very lucky."

And I am. And I know it. But any of us who take the time and the effort to discover and develop our passion—and then follow that passion—can be just as lucky.

Two-thirds of our life is spent at work or in bed; the remaining one-third is spent squeezing in everything else we want to accomplish. How are we going to spend this one-third of our life? What things will get our attention during this leisure time?

Although we can't all earn a paycheck practicing our passion, all of us choose how to spend the hours between getting off work and climbing into bed. Even those of us trapped in a less-than-joyful job have control of how we spend our free time. Knowing who we want to become, we can consciously use our leisure activities to develop our passions.

Thanks to the wonders of automation, hours on the job have decreased. We have more free time now than ever before in our nation's history. As our hours on the job have steadily decreased, technology has given us many modern conveniences—conveniences that simplify our lives, eliminating hours of labor. For many of us, microwave ovens have replaced conventional stoves, radically reducing the hours spent in meal preparation; automatic dishwashers, washing machines, and clothes dryers shorten significantly the time needed to keep dishes and clothes clean. Synthetic fabrics have eliminated most ironing, and power mowers quickly cut and mulch our grass. We now simply turn up the thermostat for more heat rather than stoke the furnace, and dump garbage into a disposal rather than make three trips a day to a pail sitting in the alley.

There's no doubt about it. We have more free time than any generation before us. The question each of us must answer is, "How am I using it?" Unless our lives are firmly fastened to our life anchors, we'll float freely with little mooring, aimlessly letting this wonderful free time slip effortlessly through our fingers.

Weekends without work are tiny packages of time that can be slowly unwrapped and savored, or rapidly ripped open and squandered. Some people face endless, empty weekends, while others juggle a calendar crammed with commitments. Joy and inner peace are possible for people at each end of this spectrum when they tightly attach their leisure activities to their personal life anchors. This attaching takes planning.

The world is filled with people who face each weekend with dread. Often, these people live alone, are dealing with a significant loss, and miss the sense of purpose and direction that going to a job gives them. When alone with "time on our hands" and nothing to do, depression wraps its arms tightly around us. We can, however, counteract and overcome its suffocating embrace by creating short-term plans that will strengthen the inner self.

Whenever I periodically face an endless, empty weekend, I prepare in advance. Knowing what inner qualities I want to strengthen, I can more easily list some short-term plans. During the weekend, I could invite a friend for supper, work on a chapter for a manuscript, read something inspirational or motivational, sit quietly in meditation, write letters to friends, or talk to my paper psychiatrist. Any, or all, of these would involve me in activities that mesh with my life anchors and would prepare me to greet Monday with a satisfying sense that I'd done something good with the weekend.

At the other end of the spectrum are all of us who find we have too much to cram into the weekend. Without some careful planning, we're going to rapidly rip the weekend to shreds and feel unfulfilled come Monday morning.

Those of us who feel our weekends are crammed with absolutely too much to do, too many appointments, meetings, dates, and obligations, can also counteract and overcome this with planning. Unless we have a clear idea of our core values, we'll be buffeted through life by every distraction and diversion that comes our way.

Develop a Passion for Paid and Unpaid Activities

Developing a passion for activities—whether we're getting paid for doing them or doing them for unpaid pleasure—we gain control of our leisure and our life. When we immerse ourselves in activities that strengthen our attentiveness, joy comes bounding into our lives.

Ask yourself, "What activities—paid and unpaid—pull me out of myself, immerse me in the moment, increase my self-confidence, and require my active participation.

Doing what we love, we can develop a passion for activities which:

+ Immerse Us in the Moment
+ Increase Our Self-Confidence
+ Require Active Participation

Choose Activities That Immerse Us in the Moment

Think of the last time you were so absorbed in an activity that you were oblivious to everything but what you were enjoying. Do you remember when you were so involved in a task or project that you stopped looking at your watch and lost yourself in the activity? Whatever you were doing probably deserves a huge hunk of your life.

I often lose track of time when I'm writing. Whether I'm writing a letter, article, lesson plan, or a manuscript, once I'm beyond the planning stage I become totally absorbed in what I'm doing. I'll be the first to admit that while I'm still incubating, trying to discover what I want to say and how I want to say it, the last thing I am is absorbed. Once I form a framework, however, for what I'm writing, once sentences jell into paragraphs and paragraphs spill into pages, I become totally oblivious to the passage of time. Suddenly I'll look out the window near my computer and notice the darkness, realizing that I've typed through the dinner hour and on into the night. Time becomes insignificant when I'm absorbed in writing.

The other activity that causes me to totally lose track of time is reading. As I was growing up, many an afternoon found me curled up in a chair or stretched out in the backyard immersed in a book. As I moved through the Bobbsey Twins, to Nancy Drew, on into the wonderful world of Laura Ingalls Wilder, I learned that reading gives insights as it entertains.

Books continue to give me strength and pleasure. Whenever I find my internal batteries need recharging, I reach for a book. In fact, I keep a book by my bed at all times and read from it nearly every night. The insights and inspiration I get from books "refill my pitcher" when my pitcher gets empty. Often, I'll start reading around nine P.M., telling myself I'll read for about an hour, and later look at the clock, discovering it's past midnight. Time becomes totally insignificant when I'm immersed in a book.

For me, learning a new computer program ranks right up there with getting a wisdom tooth pulled or having a root canal done. But my friend relishes these hours spent unraveling the hidden messages and commands inherent in each new program, enjoying the challenge so much that she loses all track of time. Because writing and teaching help her reach her life anchors—and she uses the computer for both— she's discovered a passion that fits the person she is trying to become.

Choose Activities That Increase Our Self-Confidence

If we love an activity, we'll do it more often. And the more we do it, the better we'll become at it. And the better we become, the more we want to do it. By mastering a skill, a talent, by knowing we do it rather well, we increase our passion. It's a beautifully crafted spiral, increasing our self-confidence and self-worth. We know when we have a passion for something. And we seldom have a passion for something unless we do it well.

Being an English professor and a writer, I experience the joy of loving what I do and doing what I love. But my passion for teaching and writing didn't just happen; I had to make it happen. And I had a lot of help.

Some of us discover, hone, and develop our passion on our own; most of us, however, have had a mentor, a teacher, who gave us the tools we needed and showed us that we had potential. My mentor was my eighth-grade English teacher, Lucile Knotts.

> BY MASTERING A SKILL, A TALENT, BY KNOWING WE DO IT RATHER WELL, WE INCREASE OUR PASSION

Miss Knotts had individualized instruction before its modern-day advocates were even born. After a test was given, we were allowed to let that grade stand, but few of us did. By coming in before and after school, we could take different editions of the test until we received the grade we wanted to earn. Many nights found me sitting in her classroom laboring over which form of a verb to use or whether a clause was dependent or independent. I, like hundreds of others, learned the rules backward and forward because I had to in order to do well on her tests. But what she knew, and I didn't, was that while learning for the test, I was also learning for life. By teaching me the basics of language, she gave me the tools I needed to write—then and now. In her class I discovered there were rules that made the language work. What had been an intricate puzzle was torn apart. Because I learned these basic skills in junior high, I now have the freedom to focus on *what* to say, rather than how to say it. And with that freedom I've developed a passion for the English language.

Many of us are convinced there is nothing in our lives that absorbs and immerses us, nothing that causes us to feel enthusiastic. Although we wish we had a passion for something, we often announce to the world that we don't. If that's true, it may be our own fault. And the problem may very well be that we've never repeatedly practiced something until we've mastered it.

Mastery comes through repetition; repetition requires an investment of time and energy. If we want to be good at something, we must make a commitment that, daily, for a certain number of hours, for a certain number of weeks, we'll repeatedly practice that skill. If we want to master sewing, singing, cooking, carpentering, writing, woodworking, painting, public speaking, drawing, dancing —or any skill, we'll need planned, repeated, consistent practice. All of us can master nearly anything if we're willing to invest this time and energy. Passion requires commitment. And after making that commitment to consistently practice, we may very well discover we're mastering the skill, and as sure as night follows day, we'll also discover an activity that increases our self-confidence. We'll discover our passion.

> ALL OF US CAN MASTER NEARLY ANYTHING IF WE'RE
> WILLING TO INVEST THIS TIME AND ENERGY

Choose Activities That Require Active Participation

Many activities we use to fill our hours are addictive, gobbling up entire afternoons and evenings. And the majority of these addictive activities are passive.

Without a life anchor, we'll spend these hours in idle emptiness, filling them with insignificant, passive activities, that effectively "fill up time," but fail to erase the discontent corroding the soul.

Interestingly, activities that bring inner strength usually require active participation and attentive involvement; they do not give the instant gratification that many passive activities do. And often, though not always, they are done alone, giving us an opportunity to get better acquainted with the inner self. The activities that consistently bring us joy often involve giving birth to an idea, a project, a creation, or concept. Giving birth involves our active participation. It does not occur when we're passively absorbing other people's creations; it occurs when we're making our own creations.

When we think of creation, we often think of writing, painting, sculpting, acting, or designing. Although some of us will create books, pictures, and songs, creation isn't limited to these. Each of us creates in her own authentic, unique way. Creation can be working in the garden, arranging a bowl of flowers, planning a meal, remodeling a basement, writing a journal, sewing a garment, building a swing set, repairing a car, making a loaf of bread, knitting a sweater—all of these demand active participation, all are best done alone, all require attentiveness, and all give us the opportunity to strengthen our internal resources.

Being attentive to our passion—whether we're doing it for money or doing it for pleasure—helps us be fully aware of the Now.

Live Life in Small Slices

Life can be, and often is, overwhelming. Immobilized by joyless-ness, we sometimes feel as if the pain of the past and fear of the future are squeezing all meaning out of the present moment. It doesn't have to be that way.

If I try to deal with all the pain, regrets, and losses of my past, as well as the inevitable fear of future illness, aging, and death, it's just too much. I can't do it. Rather than deal with all of life at once, I try to cut it up into little slices and deal with it just one slice at a time: one moment, one hour—at the most, one day. By living life in small slices, I'm able to concentrate only on the slice directly in front of me: Now.

Two slices of life that I've found to be vitally important are the beginning and the end of each day.

Because I've proven to myself that how I spend the first moments of each day affects my attitude and determines my joy, I use that slice of life to pinpoint qualities I want the world to see in me that day, to name people I want to influence or help. And I'm very specific: "Today I want to look for the good in each situation I'm in; to be authentic and genuine while I'm in the classroom; to plant patience in my soul. Today I want to validate Rebecca's feel-ings; to call students in each class by their name; to be a good listener when Marilyn comes for supper." Setting these little minia-ture goals helps me stay focused only on the day ahead—not the week, not the month, and certainly not my entire life.

And when the day is over and I crawl back into bed, I face another very important little slice of life: the moments before I fall asleep. After turning out the light, I thank God for all the good and positive things that have been a part of that day. I look back at the last twenty-four hours and name each and every meaningful moment that has occurred. Once again, I'm very specific: "Thank you for the letter from Aunt Ruth; thank you for the phone call from Marianne; thank you that JoAn cleaned up the coffee when I spilled it; thank you that the one o'clock class was a joy." Naming specific things I'm grateful for makes me realize that no matter what that day has been like, no matter how many problems have crept into my world, I've still got a lot of good things going for me. By repeatedly using this slice of life at the end of the day to name the good things that have occurred, I find them.

If you never have started your day setting miniature goals or ended it remembering meaningful moments, try it. You will be amazed at how it will enhance the quality of your life.

> LIFE IS A MIRROR WE LOOK INTO

Of course our lives are a mixture of both good and bad. But, sadly, some of us choose to focus our attention on only the bad, ignoring the many joyful moments that exist. To walk toward wholeness, hope, and joy, we need to consciously cultivate awareness of the good moments in our life. Like any skill, attentiveness needs to be practiced until it becomes second nature, as natural as breathing. Life is a mirror we look into. If we concentrate on and search for the good, we'll find it; if we concentrate and search for the bad, we'll find it also.

Concentrate on the Slice of Life in Front of Us: Now

Whenever some problem is squashing the joy out of me, I try, really try, to cut life into little tiny slices. Whenever I hear some fear or frustration pecking on my peace of mind, I focus my total attention on whatever I'm going to be doing the next ten minutes of my life, and I try to give those ten minutes the best Barbara I can give them. It works.

For example, I often awake in the middle of the night, my mind swirling with decisions and dilemmas. Rather than lie there for the next two hours worrying about the past or the future, I'll remind myself that for me to live in harmony with my life anchors I need good health. And I can't have good health if I don't rest. I'll say to myself, "OK, the only time that exists is Now. You can't change the past and you can't control the future, but how you spend the next moments is up to you." And then I'll reach into the memory bank of my mind, cashing in some of the deposits I've made there, letting the words of comfort and inspiration soothe my soul. Silently repeating positive, reassuring thoughts from poems, psalms, and scripture has a calming effect no tranquilizer can give. Next, I'll consciously use Herbert Benson's relaxation exercises working my way through all the muscles of my body, calming my mind as well as my body. Focusing on the Now does not assure sleep will come, but it allows me to strengthen my inner resources.

And during the day when some situation is snarling my peace of mind, I'll remind myself, "OK, you can't erase the circumstance that is pouring pain all over your day. Instead, concentrate on the next ten minutes and give them the best you've got. Focus on Now." So for the next ten minutes I concentrate on being a listener who is attentive and loving. Turning to the person I'm with, I'll consciously move my point of view from first person to second person. For those ten minutes I try to look at life through that person's eyes. What is she thinking? How is she feeling? Doing this gives me a good opportunity to practice being attentive.

Many days will find me heading toward class, thinking as I go, "God, help me for just this one hour to forget my own pain, so I can be tuned into the pain of those around me. Help me for just one hour to be positive and authentic." So do I always succeed? Am

I always able to get outside myself? Am I always positive and authentic? Of course not. But I'm always better than I would have been without attentively focusing on Now. Moving from being *I-centered* to being *you-centered* gives me inner strength. Concentrating on only the ten minutes before me, I discover that living life in small slices works.

Become a Rainbow Sprinkler; Give Ourselves Away

John Powell in *Unconditional Love* reminds us that each morning we can greet the day with either "Good morning, God!" or "Good God, morning!" When we get up, we choose whether to simply exist or to passionately throw ourselves into the day ahead. Making a conscious choice early in the morning to be energetic, enthusiastic, and pleasant, we can sprinkle rainbows over other people's days, creating joy for them and for ourselves.

We become a rainbow sprinkler by immediately putting our positive thoughts and impulses into action. When we think of something we could do that would make someone else's life more pleasant, we should do it—Now. When we think of something we could say that would make someone else's life magical and marvelous, we should say it—Now. The spontaneity, the immediacy, of following our impulses is important. If we fail to seize the moment, we'll lose both the intensity of our kindness and run the real risk of never putting our thought into action.

> ◁ WE BECOME A RAINBOW SPRINKLER BY
> IMMEDIATELY PUTTING OUR POSITIVE THOUGHTS
> AND IMPULSES INTO ACTION ▷

Ralph Waldo Emerson says, "Rings and jewels are not gifts, but apologies for gifts. The only gift is a portion of thyself." It's true. The best gift we can give another is ourselves. Mistakenly we fall into the pattern of believing that in order to give anyone a present, we must give something material: money, food, possessions. But what people really want is us, our time and our attention. If we're going to live in the Now and be a rainbow sprinkler, we'll need to become aware of all the parts of ourselves we can give as presents to other people.

Each of us has different gifts to give. We can give our time, energy, and talent. We can give appreciation, compliments, and encouragement. We can give attention, interest, and understanding. We can give smiles. We can give thank-yous. These can be given by letter, on the phone, or verbally. Every positive impulse we follow, every rainbow we sprinkle is an investment that reaps rich dividends.

We Give Ourselves Away When We Write a Letter

Letters are gifts of ourselves that we can easily give others. If we seize the moment, we'll be sending letters each time we think of someone in our present or our past who has touched our life in a special way.

If we're now grown and realize what a positive influence some teacher has had on us, it's time to get out the pen and paper and tell him. When we're young, we don't know the impact a teacher is making, but as we age, appreciation emerges. If we're thinking thanks, let's sprinkle some rainbows and put it into words. Recently I wrote my college speech teacher, telling him his dynamic, delightful lessons have continued to influence my life. I'm sure he liked receiving the letter as much as I enjoyed writing it. I've been both the giver and the receiver of these unexpected rainbows and, believe me, they're beautiful.

If our doctor is kind and caring, he or she needs to know it. We forget that medical doctors are also people—people who need positive reinforcement as much as we do. After battling pneumonia and winning the fight, I wrote a letter of thanks to my physician, not only for making me well again, but for being understanding, caring, and empathetic during the weeks of battle. Being a rainbow sprinkler means putting into words the thanks we're thinking.

If we read a book that influences our life, we can write the author a letter, telling him that what he's written has made a difference. Having received these rainbows, I can assure you that authors enjoy knowing their words have been appreciated, knowing they've made someone else's life nicer.

Recently, a clerk in one of Cincinnati's large department stores went out of her way to be helpful to me. Even though the store was swarming with Christmas shoppers, she patiently took the time to call numerous other branches of their store to find exactly the gift for which I was searching. While the glow of the moment was still fresh, upon returning home I sat at the computer and wrote the store manager, complimenting him for hiring this woman who had made my evening nicer. Following our positive impulses always creates a good feeling within us, and often does the same for the receiver.

Letters of appreciation are tiny gifts of time we can lavish on all who make our world more pleasant. If we seize the moment and follow our impulse, these letters will sprinkle rainbows over someone's day.

We Give Ourselves Away during Telephone Conversations
Telephone calls are equally easy gifts we can give. If someone has been on our mind all day, especially someone we haven't talked with for a while, perhaps we should pick up the phone and call her

—call her for absolutely no reason at all except to tell her we're glad she's our friend, we miss her, and wish we were together more often. If we seize the moment and make that phone call as soon as is humanly possible, our rainbows will be more brilliant and beautiful than if we wait until time has dampened our delight.

I recently got to experience firsthand how important it is to seize the moment and do it Now, not later. When my nephew returned to college in his late thirties, I was well aware of the financial, emotional, and physical demands it would put on both him and his wife, so when his graduation day arrived, I sent his wife a bouquet of flowers with a note saying simply, "Thanks for being the wind beneath his wings."

Now his wife could have written me a polite thank-you note after the company had left, the gifts had been opened, and the celebration was over. Instead, she picked up the phone as she was reading the card, sharing with me the immediacy of her thankfulness, the tears of her joy. By doing it Now, she let me experience her pleasure with her, sprinkling rainbows all over my day, leaving joyful tears streaming down both our cheeks.

We Give Ourselves Away When We Show Appreciation

Other presents we can give are verbal compliments and appreciation. Think of two people you would miss terribly if they were to die tonight. Whose death would rip your life to shreds, leaving a gapping, aching, empty void? How often today have you told them that you love them? Why not do it right now? Do it. Don't wait for tomorrow; tomorrow doesn't exist. The only time is NOW.

If we notice someone who looks especially nice, someone with a good-looking skirt, shirt, or haircut, we should tell her. Although we may quickly and easily do this with a good friend, we shy away from complimenting total strangers. Too often we have the thought in mind, but the words never come out of our mouths. Yet, who doesn't love to hear that something she's wearing looks nice.

If the waitress who serves us is exceptionally helpful, bubbly, and cheerful, we need to let her know we notice and appreciate being at her table. She needs to know that we're glad she entered our world today. If the tables in the restaurant are filled and her pace is harried, we can show that we understand the pressure she's working under and admire the way she's handling it. A verbal compliment means as much, often more, than the money we slip under the plate as we leave the table.

Magic occurs when we move our positive thoughts and compliments from our minds to our mouths. After giving a workshop, I make a point of thanking anyone in the audience who has given me positive feedback as I was speaking. I try to do the same in class. Recently LuAnne, a returning adult, was my student for three quarters in a row. Her presence changed the atmosphere of any class she was in. Noticing how her eyes would light up when she recognized some insight in literature, how her head would nod when she agreed or disagreed with some student, how she spontaneously laughed, joked, and smiled, I called her one night to thank her for being such a delightful addition to the class. Nods, laughs, smiles, sparkling eyes are wonderful gifts, beautiful rainbows, a listener can give a speaker. Yet, we speakers often take these gifts for granted, forgetting to say thank you to the delightful person who has given them.

And giving ourselves away doesn't always even involve words. Each time we smile at someone, we're giving away an attitude— an attitude that will have a positive influence on the person who receives our gift. When we give away a smile, we often discover the person smiles back at us, sprinkling both our worlds with rainbows.

As I work my way through the days of my life, I try to be a rainbow sprinkler. By doing so, I feel better about myself and often gain the fringe benefit of making someone else feel better also.

Choosing to stay tuned in to both ourselves and to others, we gain a new perspective on life. Being attentive to the present moment, we experience joy today—right here, right now. Making a distinction between our job and our vocation, having a passion for both work and leisure activities, living life in small slices, and being a rainbow sprinkler, we cultivate inner strength.

In the last analysis, our only freedom
is the freedom to discipline ourselves.

Bernard Baruch

PRACTICE DELAYED
GRATIFICATION

O ne of the major ingredients of inner strength is
feeling we have some control over our own destiny. And the most effective control we can have
is self control, self-discipline. Controlling our passions and
pleasures, our actions and attitudes, we no longer are leaves
in the wind blown through life by the forces of fate. Self-
discipline is an old-fashioned idea with powerful potential
—potential to strengthen the inner self, to put first things
first; potential to cultivate who we are, rather than what we
have; potential to acquire spiritual strength, rather than
"stuff and things."

> ◣ SELF-DISCIPLINE IS A POWERFUL LIFE ANCHOR, AN
> EFFECTIVE METHOD TO GAIN, TO OBTAIN, WHAT WE WANT:
> INNER STRENGTH AND JOY ◢

To many people, the word *self-discipline* has connotations of denial, deprivation, and sacrifice. To them, it means going without things they want. In essence, it's just the opposite. Self-discipline is a powerful life anchor, an effective method to gain, to obtain, what we want: inner strength and joy.

This ability to learn from the past and plan for the future is one of man's unique characteristics. In the 1940s, Dr. Robert Mowrer of Harvard conducted an experiment to determine if rats could balance long-term bad and good consequences of behavior. Pellets of food were put in front of the hungry rats. If the rats waited three seconds before eating, they received the food; if they did not wait, they received an electric shock. When the punishment occurred immediately afterward, the rats learned to wait, but if the punishment was postponed only a few additional seconds, they could not learn from it. Mowrer concluded that rats can't learn delayed gratification. Unlike rats, however, man can remember the past and plan for the future. This unique ability can be cultivated into one of his strongest life anchors.

Delayed Gratification Creates Inner Strength

Practicing delayed gratification, we weigh our present choices against what we want the final results of our lives to be; learn to say no to something we want now to gain something we want later;

give up the instant gratification of some short-term pleasure to gain the delayed gratification of a greater long-term pleasure. In the process, we strengthen a life anchor that will help us become the person we want to be. To our amazement and delight, we find joy surging into our life and splashing into the lives of those around us.

We cultivate self-discipline when we:

+ Discover We Can't Buy Joy
+ Understand We Can't Buy Others' Approval
+ Distinguish between Our Wants and Our Needs
+ Realize That We Choose How We Spend Our Money
+ Realize That We Choose How We Spend Our Time

Discover We Can't Buy Joy

In one of their essays, my students are asked to relate to their own lives the main ideas of anything they've read that quarter. The responses I get to this question are often powerful, sometimes eloquent, statements of the discontent that drains joy from their worlds. And much of this discontent is a direct result of the belief that if they had more money they could buy joy.

Discussing the short story "The Rocking Horse Winner" by D. H. Lawrence, in which a mother's expensive tastes cause their house to be haunted with the words, "There must be more money. There must be more money," students nod their heads knowingly. Because their parents have accepted our society's belief that money brings joy, many of them are living in houses that are similarly haunted.

We want joy, and we want it *now*, not in some far-distant future. Easily we fall into the instant gratification trap. Proof is abundant in our attics and our basements. Going through shelves, drawers, and boxes, many of us will find a trail of appliances that at one time we thought necessary but are now sitting unwanted and unused. Crock pots, crepe makers, coffee grinders, blenders, fondue pots, electric frying pans, pressure cookers, and woks all have had their day. But as the novelty and newness wore off, many were stashed away in a hidden corner of some cupboard.

Seeking instant gratification, we've all purchased items, only to find our fascination for them was fleeting. Buying the latest adult toy, we discovered that the initial delight brought by the new VCR, compact disc player, stereo system, computer, digital camera, large-screen TV, or camcorder was short-lived. These technological toys we once thought were perfect quickly grew commonplace and out-dated. But, wait. There's a new toy on the market now, a toy that's faster, bigger, and better, a toy that will undoubtedly make us joy-ful. So we buy it—only to discover it soon has to be replaced by a newer and more expensive model.

Even though possessions fail repeatedly to bring joy into our lives, we're convinced that eventually they will. But if we only look around us, we can see they won't. If possessions created joy, we who live in the twenty-first century should certainly be more joyous than people who lived in the middle of the twentieth.

In the 1950s, the majority of families each had one car, one tele-vision, and one telephone; now the majority have two (or more) cars, two (or more) televisions, and two (or more) telephones. Today, garbage disposals, automatic clothes dryers, microwave ovens, and air conditioners are often considered necessities. Yet for many years, I and millions of others lived meaningful lives without owning any of these. Without question, our society has more mate-rial possessions today than it had fifty years ago. You'd think we'd be brimming over with joy. But we're not.

> ⚐ EVEN THOUGH POSSESSIONS FAIL REPEATEDLY TO
> BRING JOY INTO OUR LIVES, WE'RE CONVINCED
> THAT EVENTUALLY THEY WILL ⚑

As affluence has increased, there has been no corresponding jump in the level of joy or inner strength in people's lives. On the contrary, statistics show that suicide, alcoholism, drug abuse, homicides, and depression have increased dramatically since the '50s.

Choosing to ignore the lack of correlation between affluence and joy, many of us persist in our pursuit of material possessions. Once we know that who we are is more important than what we have, there is no longer a need to stay on this financial treadmill. And we get off. Self-discipline keeps us off.

Understand We Can't Buy Others' Approval

We often try to buy other people's approval as well as self-approval, hoping we can convince others as well as ourselves that we're worth something.

Diane, divorced and living alone, was, for many years, always going financially backward. During our friendship, we often talked about the lack of joy in her life—a lack she felt was caused by never having enough money.

Considering bankruptcy, she came over one night to talk to me about her options. "The balance due on all my credit cards is bigger than my yearly take-home pay. I'm getting nowhere fast," lamented Diane. "I'm digging a deeper and deeper hole for myself, and I honestly don't know how to get out." After listening to her, listing all her debts, expenses, and income, I saw that the problem was not lack of money.

Although working full-time, Diane consistently spent more than she made. "Why not tear up the credit cards and quit spending money you don't have?" I asked. This was not an option she wanted to consider. "I know it's the right thing to do, but I can't do it. I need to buy things to feel I've got something to show for being alive. To quit buying would be like dying," she answered.

Realizing her lack of delayed gratification was grounded in some emotional hole she was trying to fill, I urged her to start talking to a psychologist. Only by knowing the cause could she confront and deal with it. She followed my suggestion.

After seeing a psychologist regularly for many months, Diane saw what she was doing to herself. Although it was a slow and sometimes painful process, this awareness brought the self-discipline she sought. Being a daughter of an alcoholic mother, she'd always felt she was "not as good as" other people. In order to gain the approval she sought, she had purchased items, knowing full well that she couldn't pay for them. Although having unpaid debts was hard, feeling she was worthless was even harder. Because of what they symbolized, the possessions were more important to her than the debt. Lacking self-confidence and self-awareness, Diane had been attempting to buy people's approval—approval she'd never gotten from her mother. Once she saw the dynamics of what she was doing, her need to purchase possessions lessened. Instant gratification no longer ruled her; she saw she had a choice. Once she reached this understanding, she found she no longer needed to purchase people's approval. She now had something much more important: self-approval.

Distinguish between Our Wants and Our Needs

Money—in and of itself—certainly isn't bad. But we need to be aware of what it can and can't do. It can pay for our needs, but it can't begin to satisfy our wants.

Our needs are few; our wants are many. Learning to distinguish between actual needs and perceived wants increases the level of joy in our lives. It's more difficult, however, to make this distinction than it used to be. Using credit cards, we easily fall into the trap of transforming wants into needs. Desiring has become getting; spending has replaced saving. And getting and spending have become the American way of life. Confusing our wants with our needs, we crave the unattainable, wish for things we can't afford and don't need.

> LEARNING TO DISTINGUISH BETWEEN ACTUAL NEEDS AND PERCEIVED WANTS INCREASES THE LEVEL OF JOY IN OUR LIVES

Written in the nineteenth century, Wordsworth's words, "The world is too much with us; late and soon,/Getting and spending, we lay waste our powers," foretold the instant gratification treadmill of the twenty-first century. Failing to distinguish between our wants and our needs, buying things we can't afford, we deplete our inner selves.

Stepping on the instant gratification treadmill, we "lay waste our powers," using our time and energy "getting and spending" rather than strengthening the inner self. We're using precious moments, magic hours, yearning for material objects that are only wants, not needs. Desiring instant gratification, we purchase these objects, only to find ourselves using additional moments and hours dusting, washing, drying, and cleaning what we've purchased. Using our time and energy desiring, purchasing, and caring for material objects, rather than caring for the inner self, we're committing spiritual suicide.

Knowing that what's important is who we are, not what we have, lessens our wants, making us more content. Self-discipline becomes easier; our financial lifestyles change, and we no longer feel deprived when we can't purchase what we formerly craved. Realizing possessions not only won't create joy but often hinder its arrival, we begin simplifying our lives, ridding ourselves of all the "stuff and things" that clutter our soul. Slowly, thoughtfully, we start throwing away, cleaning out, and eliminating everything that junks up our lives. Living in harmony with our life anchors, we discover we actually desire fewer possessions.

For Many, Cable TV and Caller ID Have Become Needs

Unless we're consciously trying to strengthen the inner self, however, the difference between needs and wants becomes blurred by the little plastic card we painlessly pull out to make purchases. My students know this is true.

Rachel, a former student, once wrote, "There's no way my husband and I can live a decent life. We just don't make enough money. We're broke, always broke. I'm sick and tired of not being able to pay the bills." She then told how they carried a constant balance of around $5,000 on one credit card, $3,000 on another, and owed every utility company in Cincinnati.

Later, Rachel came in to talk to me about the essay. After we'd discussed her writing skills, she turned to me and said, "You know it's true. We just don't make enough money. We can only make the minimum payment on the credit cards. The interest just keeps increasing." Sensing her frustration, I asked, "What caused you to get into so much debt?" "Oh, you know. Just stuff we really needed," she replied.

It turned out they "needed" a king-size waterbed, two televisions, a Walkman, a VCR, an answering machine, an audiocassette player, and a cordless telephone. I later learned that they were eating at fast-food restaurants three nights a week, paying for caller ID and cable television each month, and buying pizza and renting videos each weekend.

It wasn't that they couldn't "live a decent life" because they "didn't make enough money." It was simply that they'd chosen to spend more money than they made. They failed to realize that eating fast food and pizza each week, paying for cable TV and caller ID each month, and renting video movies constantly were robbing them of joy. Confusing wants with needs, they'd "purchased" every item they desired—and a mountain of debt.

We Choose How We Spend Our Money

When spending money, we'll want to ask ourselves, "What's important?" "What's my bottom line in life?" "Will this use of money strengthen those qualities that will help me become the person I want to be?"

The headlines scream: "Everyone But the Rich Feels Strapped," "Middle-Income Americans Can't Make Ends Meet," "Modern Family Has Trouble Living on One Income." Bombarded by these beliefs, we fall for them, even when they aren't always true. Many of these people who "feel strapped," "can't make ends meet," and "have trouble living on one income," aren't poor. They simply spend more than they make. Although they say, "I can't afford . . ." these words often mean, "I've chosen to spend that money on other wants."

While in my freshman English class, Stephanie told me in one of her essays, "We've got so many bills that we can't pay our health insurance premium this month because the bank balance is zero." Yet, in the same essay I was told they had a large-screen TV, a hot tub, a cellular phone, a compact disc player, a VCR, a camcorder, and a computer. She also described the numerous videos her husband had purchased for their collection, as well as the compact discs and computer software she'd just bought. As I read the essay, I thought, "It's not that you don't have enough money to pay the health insurance premium this month; it's that you've chosen to spend the money on other things in previous months."

> ◈ LIFE DOESN'T MAKE US POOR; WE MAKE OURSELVES POOR BY THE CHOICES WE MAKE ✍

Stephanie and her husband's take-home pay was over $4,000 a month. They weren't poor; they were members of a generation who, when hearing CD, think of compact disc, not certificate of deposit.

What's more important? Our health or technological toys? Stephanie's statement showed that a compact disc player, a VCR, a camcorder, a computer, as well as CDs, videos, film, and computer software, were more important to them than health insurance. Choices, not lack of money, were making them joyless.

This couple reminds me of some of the students in my colleague's classes. Teaching speech, a class where listening as well as speaking is taught, she emphasizes the importance of attendance. Knowing that emergencies always occur, she tells her students on the first day that they have five excused absences for illness and unexpected emergencies. They are warned repeatedly not to use these excused days until they're needed—yet they do. Rather than save those days for illness or an emergency, they use them for their convenience—to sleep in, to shop, to watch soap operas, to cram for a test in another course. Then they get the flu, and all their excused days have been used up. Loudly they blame my colleague for not excusing them "for being sick," rather than blame themselves for choosing to spend those excused days on things other than illness.

Like Stephanie, many of my students believe they have no choices concerning money. They are obsessed with trying to pay the bills, always wanting more money, never having enough. They think they are trapped.

But they aren't trapped, and neither are we. We have choices: We can choose to be frugal savers, or we can choose to be consummate consumers. "It isn't what you earn—it's what you *save* that makes you rich," said Francis Bacon in the seventeenth century. The wisdom of his words still holds true. Life doesn't make us poor; we make ourselves poor by the choices we make.

We Choose How We Spend Our Time

My students have problems not only making positive choices concerning money; they also have an ongoing problem with choices concerning time.

Clara, one of my students, called last week to tell me that she'd have to hand in her out-of-class essay late. She explained that although she'd tried to work on it each night for over a week, life was closing in around her, leaving no time to write the paper. Filtering down through her words was a feeling of busyness, pressure, and fast pace. She was taking two classes, working twenty-four hours a week at a bank, taking care of her two boys, cleaning the house, preparing the meals, and running never-ending errands. She was perpetually exhausted.

As I listened, I thought, "She's trying to squash too much into too few hours. And she's at the breaking point." I then suggested that perhaps over the quarter break she could slow down, catch her breath, and regroup. But no, Clara had already told the bank that during the Christmas break she would work full-time. She explained, "This will give us money we need to pay some of the bills and buy Christmas presents. With Matt working overtime each week and me working full-time for three weeks, we'll bring home really good paychecks." "And will working over the break make you less exhausted?" I asked. "Well, no," she replied. "But it will give us money." They were chasing money with an intensity that left no time for cultivating their inner selves.

> WE CAN CHOOSE OUR LEVEL OF JOY BY PRACTICING SELF-DISCIPLINE AND DELAYED GRATIFICATION

I questioned her, "Why are you two doing this? Don't tell me; tell each other. Once you know why Matt is working fifty hours a week and why you want to work full-time during vacation, you'll know what you're putting first in your lives." I reminded her, "This is your life, and you only get one chance to live it. These years will never, never come back. You'll never be this age again; Matt will never be this age again; your boys will never be this age again. Life doesn't allow reruns. If this pace is what you both want, fine. But I question if it really is." Since only a few weeks earlier we'd had a class discussion on life anchors and what's important, I suggested that she and her husband try to list their life anchors and see if they were spending their time in harmony with those anchors.

A few nights later I answered the phone to hear Clara's voice. "We did what you suggested. We listed the things that are really important to us, the qualities we want to develop in ourselves. And nearly every single thing we thought of went back to relationships and love. We'd listed staying in good health, being positive role models as parents, having a marriage with open communication, and raising physically, emotionally, and spiritually healthy boys. What an eye-opener making that list was!"

"By choosing to fill our time with too many things, we aren't living in harmony with any of our life anchors! And we're going to change that," she continued. "Who needs lots of toys if we're not healthy! Who needs material possessions if our marriage is falling apart! Who needs money if our children aren't getting the attention they crave. I'm not taking the full-time job over the break; I'm going to spend that time getting reacquainted with my family."

All the Dianes, Rachels, Stephanies, and Claras who are drowning in discontent have a choice. We all have a choice. We can choose our level of joy by practicing self-discipline and delayed gratification. Then we'll find we agree with Thoreau when he says, "A man is rich in proportion to the number of things which he can afford to let alone."

Self-Discipline Is Easiest Learned Early in Life

When life is joyless, we're tempted at times to delete the discomfort by reaching for the instant gratification of some possession, pleasure, or passion. Knowing that self-discipline will help us focus on what's really important, we begin consciously disciplining ourselves, only to discover that what sounds so easy on paper is darned difficult in practice. And we find ourselves asking, "Why can some people delay gratification so much more easily than others?"

They can because they've had more practice. Delaying our gratification for material possessions as well as for food, alcohol, sex, cigarettes, and every other pleasure and passion that entices us is learned. And some of us had better teachers than others. Part of the skill of delayed gratification is learning to experience—and live through—the disappointment and sorrow of not always getting what we want when we want it. If as children we experienced grief and disappointment in small increments, we now have a valuable skill for handling the vast varieties of sorrow that enter our lives. We have the inner strength to face life's dirty deals rather than run for the nearest, easiest exit. If throughout the years we've repeatedly practiced delayed gratification and we've *gained something positive* in the process, self-discipline has become a learned skill. Success breeds success. Once we've experienced the positive results, the skill becomes easier; with years of practice the skill becomes almost automatic. And the earlier we begin, the better.

What we did as children and teens formed the foundation for what we do now. How we handled little things when young often influences how we'll respond to later, larger issues. If, as children, we ate the vegetable we disliked before we ate the mashed potatoes we loved; if we ate the outside trim off a piece of cinnamon toast before we ate the center; if we ate the cake first and saved the thickest icing for last; if we ate the crust off the back of a piece of pie before eating the filling—we laid the first tiny beginning bricks in a foundation for future delayed gratification. If, as children, we did our homework before we went outside to play; if we put money into savings before we bought the desired jeans; if we cleaned our room before going to the party; if we wrote the thank-you note before using the gift—we continued laying bricks in a foundation that would become more solid as we aged.

Chances are great that, as adults, we now do the chores we most dislike before the ones we enjoy; make the dreaded phone call before making the enjoyable one; pay the savings account before paying the monthly bills; write the minutes for the meeting before reading the mystery novel.

Although we adults can't change what we absorbed from our parents, we certainly can choose what our children will absorb from us. We can help them cultivate the inner strength that comes from self-discipline by letting them experience grief in small increments. It's very difficult to watch a disappointed child; it's much easier to give him what he wants when he wants it. Trying to hold disappointment at bay, we sometimes coddle and comfort children who could be made stronger if we'd only allow ourselves the temporary discomfort of watching them experience short-term pain.

We Are Reluctant to Say No to Material Wants

By giving instant gratification, we make our lives easier for the short-term: no longer do we have to see the child grief-stricken because he doesn't have designer jeans; sorrowful because he can't have the eighty-dollar pair of gym shoes; angry because he isn't the proud possessor of the latest video game system. Rather than go through this short-term grief, it's easier to buy the item.

If children learn they can "push the right buttons" and get what they want when they want it, they'll have a hard time dealing with life's later, greater disappointments—disappointments that no amount of "pushing the right buttons" will eliminate or eradicate.

If a child loses her favorite toy, she's devastated. Rather than letting her hurt for a while, we'll often immediately buy a replacement. But by doing so, we've missed one of those precious opportunities for allowing her to experience loss in small increments, learning in tiny steps to deal with this emotion that is going to fade in and out of the remainder of her life.

We Are Reluctant to Say No to Adult Pleasures

Another way we can help our children gain the inner strength that comes from self-discipline is to say no to some of their desired adult pleasures. Because the credit card has made it possible for many young people to get whatever they want whenever they want it, the distinction between having something now and having something later has been blurred to such an extent that it sometimes spills over into other aspects of their lives, and wanting to *have* things now becomes wanting to *do* things now. Once again, some parents find it difficult to make a clear distinction between instant and delayed gratification.

Shopping at one of Cincinnati's large department stores, I took my place with others waiting to pay for purchases. Standing in line beside me, a father and his young daughter were having an animated discussion concerning her desire to wear lipstick. "But Daddy, you don't understand," she pleaded. "I'm in the fourth grade now; I'm not a child. Do you want me to be the only girl in the whole class who doesn't wear lipstick? If everyone else does, can't I?" Expecting to hear a masculine voice reply, "No. Not until you're older," I heard instead, "Oh, I guess it's OK if everyone else is wearing it."

While eating in an exquisite restaurant recently, I was enjoying the beauty of the surroundings: fresh flowers, white tablecloths, soft piano music, candlelight, and gourmet food. As I was feasting on both the food and the atmosphere, I noticed a family of four sitting at a table nearby: mom, dad, and two young daughters—one looked about four years old and the other perhaps six. When I overheard the six-year-old demand lobster for her dinner, the whole scene seemed out of focus. Although their parents could probably afford paying thirty dollars for each child's dinner, doing so seemed unfair to the children. As those girls move into adulthood, one of their rites of passage will not be that first awe-filled visit to an elegant restaurant. By not encouraging delayed gratification, these adults were helping to create future teens who would feel they were entitled to such restaurants as well as other adult pleasures and passions that would be more wisely saved "for later."

Our Reluctance to Say No Spawns Joylessness

Failure to say no to children is usually done for our benefit, not the child's. Attempting to fill some huge hole within our inner selves, we purchase and protect, even when doing so harms the child.

Growing out of our need to be a pleaser or our own feelings of guilt, self-sacrifice becomes easier than saying no. Attempting to give the child whatever she wants, a parent may either be trying to buy the affection he didn't get as a child or he may be trying to appease the guilt that results from not spending enough time with the child. Divorced, single, or double-income parents can easily tumble into this trap, yet children would rather have our time and attention than toys and trinkets. This indulgence in material possessions produces selfish, never-satisfied, joyless adults. When a child who has seldom heard no enters the adult world, which repeatedly tells all of us no, he'll rebel each time he can't experience instant gratification. And will he thank you? No.

As adults, these children who have never learned to delay gratification won't say: "I'm so happy you never said no to me. I'm so glad you turned your world upside down to give me whatever I wanted." Joy will be light years away when this adult child has an overdrawn back account, falls behind on his car payments, and can't pay back his student loans. There will be little joy in his life when he's overweight, in debt, or on drugs. Joy will not permeate the home when he gets his first DUI, is suspended from college for cheating, or repeatedly gets speeding tickets.

If a child doesn't know sorrow at a superficial level, when she hits adulthood, she'll be unable to deal with the significant sorrow that is an integral part of being human. Life will place roadblocks in her path; some of those roadblocks will require delaying gratification, using self-discipline. As an adult, she'll quickly find out she can't have everything she wants whenever she wants it.

Parents Can Encourage Delayed Gratification

Ideally, our parents help us take those first faltering steps toward self-discipline. Practicing delayed gratification themselves, they influence us at an almost subliminal level. Raising us with consistent love and discipline, they plant the seeds for delayed gratification—seeds that will harvest and bloom into joy as we reach adulthood. Trusting us to emulate their actions, they are seldom disappointed. If they trust us to handle time, money, sex, and food, we gain self-confidence in our abilities. By creating this trust and self-confidence throughout infancy and childhood, they help us learn the joy of self-control.

The quicker parents move from control, to influence, to trust, the more joy there will be in everyone's life.

I was fortunate to be raised by two parents who gave me this trust. Never having a curfew, I knew I was trusted to have enough sense to come in at a decent hour. And I did. Giving me a checking account and a budget book when I was sixteen, they continued to trust me. I was told, "You're on your own. Pay savings before you spend; keep track of what you spend. When you're spending faster than you can keep track, you know you're spending too much." Although I purchased things that were definitely luxuries, I knew the responsibility for my finances was mine. Knowing that if I didn't buy those four ten-dollar dresses (Remember, this was the '50s!) I wanted, I soon learned that I could later buy that absolutely stunning forty-dollar one I craved. Knowing that it was my certificate of deposit, not theirs, that would be purchased with the money I saved, I found that watching interest accumulate was more enjoyable than spending money.

Knowing I was trusted concerning my teenage sexual activity, self-discipline learned to rule desire. Difficult as it was, I well remember jumping up and walking across the room when passion could easily have overwhelmed me, destroying not only my own joy, but my parents' and my boyfriend's as well. Knowing that I was trusted to eat the right foods and stay healthy, I found it a challenge to live up to their trust. Realizing if I delayed the satisfaction of high-calorie foods at lunch that I could have more pleasure when I ate dinner, I learned to control my passion for food.

Believing and trusting, my parents gave me the freedom I needed to develop self-confidence. But they didn't do this by controlling me; they didn't do it with rules and regulations. Rather, by giving me consistent trust and practicing delayed gratification themselves, they allowed self-discipline to seep into my life by osmosis. Because of them, delayed gratification was easy to practice. I'm a very lucky woman.

Knowing Our Life Anchors, We Practice Delayed Gratification

We adults choose at a conscious or unconscious level to opt for short-term pain/long-term gain or short-term gain/long-term pain. And the foundation for this choice is often laid in childhood. Adults who quickly "cut and run" from short-term pain often are those who have watched family members do the same.

Of course it's easier to "cut and run" when the going gets bad. Lacking skill in delayed gratification, whenever new problems arise, we quickly leave our marriages, our jobs, our apartments, our towns. "Moving on" is always the easy answer; it isn't always the best one. Those who take the easy route have often had parents who couldn't bear to let them encounter life's little losses when they were children.

So, shall we all blame our parents because we have trouble delaying gratification? Is it their fault that we eat, drink, and spend too much? Of course not. Our parents did the best they could at the time they raised us. That was then; this is now. Blaming our parents is a sure way to stay stuck in joylessness.

If our parents lacked the knowledge, ability, or desire to encourage delayed gratification, we'll have to teach ourselves; if our parents failed to put people before possessions, we'll have to rearrange our priorities by ourselves. Taking small baby steps, we can keep our eyes fastened on our long-term life goals; we can practice saying no to purchases, places, and people that will keep us from reaching

> ❧ LACKING SKILL IN DELAYED GRATIFICATION, WHENEVER NEW PROBLEMS ARISE, WE QUICKLY LEAVE OUR MARRIAGES, OUR JOBS, OUR APARTMENTS, OUR TOWNS ❧

those goals. Delayed gratification tempers us and makes us stronger. Just as we temper steel to give it strength and staying power, we can temper ourselves. Having a clear vision of where we want our lives to head lessens the obsession with instant gratification.

If, however, we've had controlling rather than trusting parents, if we've had authoritarian rather than loving parents, we'll have a harder time learning delayed gratification. That's not to say we can't do it; it simply means we'll have to work harder at it than those fortunate few who learned self-discipline as children and teenagers. Nevertheless, once we've experienced the good feeling of knowing we can go without something now in order to gain something later, we realize we can control the level of joy in our life. That realization is something a person doesn't easily relinquish.

Knowing what's important—what inner qualities we want to develop—makes it easier to temper ourselves, easier to cultivate self-discipline as a life anchor. Knowing that who we are is more important than what we have, we find that instant gratification becomes easier to sacrifice and self-discipline easier to practice.

We live in deeds, not years; in thoughts, not breaths;
In feelings, not in figures on a dial.
We should count time by heart-throbs.
He most lives who thinks most, feels the noblest,
acts the best.
Life's but a means unto an end; that end
Beginning, mean, and end to all things—God.

Philip James Bailey, "A Country Town"

◀ 10 ▶

CULTIVATE HOPE AND FAITH

I absentmindedly picked up the next essay on the pile, read it, graded it, and cried. The student, a returning adult, had written, "Living makes absolutely no sense. People's lives have more bad than good, more sorrow than happiness, more selfishness than kindness. Why should I, or any other human, continue living in this meaningless world?

If you can give me any reason I shouldn't kill myself, I want you to write it at the end of this essay."

Sitting there, essay in hand, I thought, "God, why me? Of all the people she could have asked who would have known what to say, why me? I'm getting too many of these pleas."

When their lives rip apart at the seams, my students reach out to me, searching for some reason to go on living, some reason to "keep on keeping on." Reaching down inside themselves, trying to find that reason, they come up empty-handed. Seeing my wheelchair, sensing that there must have been times in my life when I've had to "keep on keeping on," their internal radar tells them I just might understand what they're going through.

Learning long ago to take these comments seriously, I turned the essay over and responded. I knew she didn't want professional advice; she simply wanted me to know that she was at the end of her string. My job as her teacher was to validate her despair, offer a listening ear, and see that she was getting psychological counseling.

Listing all the reasons I could think of why a person might choose to continue living, I realized that all of them had roots in my own personal faith, that we are a part of a scheme of things larger than our own miniature, messed-up world. As I was writing, I kept thinking, "Everything goes back to having a solid spiritual core—a core that helps us see that we're valuable, unique, and important. Without that spiritual core, that faith in something larger than ourselves, it's hard for anyone to find meaning in life."

And many of my students do not have that faith.

As I compare my students of today with those I sat beside in the '50s and taught in the '60s, I hear a hollow ring in their inner selves that was not as prevalent forty years ago. We're materially rich and spiritually poor.

The last four decades have been marked by an insatiable pursuit of pleasure and possessions. Although our homes are filled with more gadgets, toys, and luxuries than those of any other generation before us, our inner lives often remain empty, joyless, and unfulfilled. Both teens and adults fill our mental health clinics and hospitals, struggling with this inner emptiness that fills every fiber of modern society. Lacking a satisfying sense of who we are and what we're living for, we remain joyless.

Faith Is the Foundation for Joy

We can stop blaming our past, control our attitudes and habits, move outside our self-centeredness, allow ourselves to be authentic, live life in the Now, and practice delayed gratification—and *still* find ourselves joyless, unless our life anchors grow out of and reflect a faith in a power higher than ourselves. In order to get through life's trials and know they're worth getting through, we need to know that our being alive matters. We need to believe that what's going on inside us is much more important than what's going on around us.

Immersed in the routine of daily chores, we're too busy living to question why we're alive. But then some life event suddenly whirls us around and forces us to consider what's really important in life: We work our way through a wrenching divorce; we suffer the death of a spouse; we're told our daughter has been paralyzed in a car wreck. Facing a crisis forces us to face our inherent spirituality, which has been tugging at our souls but previously got carefully swept under our "to do" lists and our datebooks. Our days and nights are suddenly spent asking, "What's important?"

Such a crisis recently walked into my life. Waking one morning and discovering I couldn't sit up in bed, waves of panic and pain washed over me. If I couldn't sit up, I couldn't catheterize myself, get out of bed, get dressed, or be independent. Lying helplessly in bed with only a phone between me and the rest of the world, I experienced an entrapment such as I've not experienced for over forty years. That morning began weeks of being immobilized by acute neuritis in a major back muscle. Suddenly this paraplegic was reminded that the only thing keeping her from being a quadriplegic were those critical muscles between T7 and the top of her back—and her entire physical independence centered on the ability of those crucial muscles to work. And for weeks they wouldn't.

Working my way through that crisis, I kept asking myself, "How can I use this rotten mess to strengthen my life anchors? What can I think, do, and say that will help me grow from this?" As I reached into the crevices of my inner self, I had a beautiful spiritual awakening. One night as I was repeating the Twenty-third Psalm, I stopped at the line: "He maketh me to lie down in green pastures." Always amazed at the levels of symbolism inherent in the psalms, I thought, "Why the verb *maketh*?" It wasn't *requests*, or *asks*, or *suggests*. It was *maketh*. And I wrestled with the significance of that verb. Life had *made* me "lie down." Symbolically, the psalm was saying by forcing me to lie down, I'd find nourishment and sustenance: green pastures. How? How in the name of heaven could being forced into the immobility of this entrapped existence give me nourishment and sustenance? Believing each of life's experiences is an opportunity for spiritual growth, I started asking and answering the question, "Why am I alive?" Reaffirming my personal, positive life anchors strengthened my faith in God and my hope for the future.

Each of Us Is Unique and Valuable

If we ask "Why am I alive?" and have no clue, we may very well find ourselves asking the same question my student did at the end of her essay: "Why live?"

Faith in God gives us a desire not only to live, but to live well. Unless we believe our being alive makes the world a better place, we're going to have a hard time getting in touch with our spiritual core; unless we have faith in our own uniqueness, we'll find it difficult to have faith in a power higher than ourselves.

Each time we successfully face and survive personal trauma, we increase our belief that we have value, that we are unique, that we are a reflection of the God within. This faith in our personal spiritual value gives us staying power when life hands us rotten reality. This staying power does not lessen our pain, our fear, or our sorrow; it does, however, give us the steel inner strength to claw our way through that rotten reality, not *over* it, not *around* it, but *through* it. It's the coming through that makes us know we have value—and that value is closely tied to our personal theology of life.

As spiritually maturing people, we accept the paradoxical elements of the human condition—a human condition filled with both good and bad. Spirituality does not give us a snug, safe, sheltered haven of certainty; rather, it offers us the strength to live with uncertainty. In the midst of life's dirty deals, spiritual people are less likely to crumble. Joy is struggling, questioning, searching for inner strength—and finding it in the midst of the ambiguities of life.

> THIS FAITH IN OUR PERSONAL SPIRITUAL VALUE GIVES US STAYING POWER WHEN LIFE HANDS US ROTTEN REALITY

Whenever we're living in harmony with our life anchors, whenever we're deliberately strengthening our loving, life-affirming qualities, whenever we're reaching outside our own little world to make someone else's world better, we know we're making a difference—to ourselves and to others. Achieving this harmony, you and I profoundly affect the lives we touch each day. Seeing our faith in our own uniqueness and spirituality increases other people's belief in their own. In a world where strength and courage are craved, we add our tiny portion. As spiritual, introspective, reflective people, we do make a significant difference in the world. Saying yes to our life anchors, we're also saying yes to our God.

Modern Society Clings to Substitutes for Faith

Searching for a faith that transcends the problems of daily life—searching for a faith that helps us become spiritual, introspective, and reflective—has led some people to misuse both religion and psychology.

Strands of reality, as well as perceived reality, have woven themselves together to weaken and sometimes strangle our faith in any power higher than ourselves. When we see corruption within some organized religion, pious people spewing hatred, and pop psychologists preaching self-centered salvation, we wince, wondering if the spiritual connectedness we crave is a mirage. It isn't if we can see the relationship between spiritual and religious.

Whereas *religious* means "characterized by adherence to a religion," *spiritual* means "of the spirit or the soul" (*Webster's New World Dictionary*). For most people, *religious* carries connotations of organized religion, while *spiritual* does not. Because a spiritual person is "filled with the spirit," religious people can be spiritual and spiritual people can be religious.

It's possible to be spiritual and not religious—difficult, perhaps, but possible. Logically, it would be impossible, however, to be religious and not spiritual. Because an organized group, a community of believers, has the strong advantage of giving us a sense of belonging, a needed feeling of connectedness, organized religion usually enlarges and enriches our spiritual life. Unfortunately, in the real world that's not always the case.

If the act of attending services becomes more important than our relationship with our God and his people, we're not being spiritual; if images become more important than essence, we're not being spiritual; if we leave the principles and precepts of our religion at the altar as we walk out the door, we're not being spiritual.

When People Misuse Religion, They Give Faith a Bad Name

Seeing extreme right-wing conservatives preaching their faith of exclusion, priests sexually abusing young men, the Ku Klux Klan urging white supremacy, televangelists conning the audience out of money to pay for their own lavish living, we may question the integrity of anyone who calls himself religious.

The six P.M. news screams that there is corruption within the church. Stories of religious people failing to be spiritual drag on for weeks, with the TV audience hanging onto each word and pronouncing all religion corrupt. TV, newspapers, and magazines use these deviant religious leaders' lives to twist our concept of faith and spirituality, giving us a distorted picture. These stories stand out for the very reason that they are aberrant behavior. Problems within the organized church make good copy. Social ills are played up because they are *not* the norm. That's why they're news.

We readers and viewers realize our news is the deviant, not the norm, but we forget. We may say, "If religious people are like that, I want no part of religion." All religious people are not like that. These stories that fill our family rooms are the exception, the atypical. They cause us to forget the thousands of dedicated, dynamic spiritual leaders, as well as the millions of devoted laypeople within all organized religions.

When People Misuse Psychology, They Give Faith a Bad Name

Finding that some deviant members of organized religion have let us down, we reach for modern-day substitutes—substitutes that end up making each of us the center of our own little universe. Trying to get that sense of connectedness we crave, we blindly follow the myriad of New-Age gurus telling us we can fill the spiritual void in our lives if we'll only increase the faith we have in ourselves, if we'll only increase our self-esteem.

Knowing this coveted self-esteem is a by-product of our choices, skills, actions, attitudes, and abilities, on the first day of the fall quarter I tell my university students that I'm not going to "bolster their self-esteem" by giving their essays higher grades than they've earned, putting happy faces on their papers, or praising them for sloppy work. Because these practices have been used in their past schooling, students are surprised, yet pleased. They know when teachers are authentic, and they know when praise is hollow and undeserved. I tell them, "You'll acquire self-esteem when you master a subject, when you learn a skill, when you increase your ability. Self-esteem is not something that anyone gives you; it is a by-product of how you live."

What's true in the classroom is true for us. Self-esteem is not something that someone hands us; it's the result of a life well-lived.

Yet for some people, this pop psychology is replacing organized religion, moving us from faith in a power higher than ourselves to faith in personal self-fulfillment. The spiritual lives of many joyless people are built on this shaky, shifting narcissistic faith of self-esteem. The New-Age pop psychologists tell us if we only repeat enough positive affirmations, we'll have all the faith and hope we need. There are now hundreds of books and tapes filled with uplifting affirmations with which we can begin each day. And they're being purchased as fast as they're printed. People hunger for faith and hope. Traditional daily devotions, with which religious people have begun their days for centuries, are now being replaced with these daily affirmations. Building self-esteem has become society's current panacea for spiritual emptiness.

> ✎ SELF-ESTEEM IS NOT SOMETHING THAT SOMEONE HANDS US; IT'S THE RESULT OF A LIFE WELL-LIVED ✎

Listening to self-affirmation tapes and reading books to bolster self-esteem leave us empty and unfulfilled. Rather than attempting to build self-esteem, perhaps we should concentrate on increasing our self-worth. Although people often fail to distinguish between these words, *self-esteem* is not a synonym for *self-worth*.

In the searching for self-esteem, we focus on ourselves, on what feels good, on what makes us happy. Each of us is the center of our own little universe. In contrast, self-worth occurs when we make moral, ethical, and spiritual choices that are closely tied to our life anchors. We'll have self-worth as we make a positive difference in the lives of the people around us. Self-worth is a by-product of a life lived purposefully connected to our faith.

> ◁ TRYING TO MAKE OURSELVES THE CENTER OF THE
> UNIVERSE, WE'LL CONTINUE CRAVING CONNECTION TO A
> FAITH THAT TRANSCENDS OUR OWN TINY WORLDS ▷

According to the modern-day soothsayers, we can project our way to wondrous wealth, rapturous relationships, and solid self-esteem. According to them, we can affirm our way to faith.

It won't work. Positive affirmations based on only the inner self will be meaningless unless that inner self is tuned to God. Trying to make ourselves the center of the universe, we'll continue craving connection to a faith that transcends our own tiny worlds.

We Humans Tend to Make Our God Too Small

Without this faith that transcends the self, we'll feel disconnected, because humans have, I believe, an inherent spirituality, an intrinsic thirst for connectedness, an ingrained pull toward a power higher than themselves. We call this power God. Each of us will have a slightly different concept of who or what this God is. And that's all right. The spirituality that leads us toward our God encompasses basic precepts that span across religions.

Living in an age of religious relativism, we've reduced many ideas of right and wrong to personal taste, leaving our children and teens, as well as some adults, floating through life with no spiritual anchor. Living in a country that encourages private religious beliefs, we've created myriad competing religions, religions that divide and exclude more often than they join and include.

Consciously getting in touch with our spiritual core makes us aware that the differences existing as a result of religious relativism and individual beliefs need not leave us anchorless, need not destroy our faith. As various religions, sects, and denominations stress their differences from other religions, sects, and denominations, too often they tear to shreds the basic precepts upon which they were founded. Walking the journey toward joy, cultivating our faith, we'll discover it doesn't have to be this way.

Perhaps one reason this has happened is because we all have a tendency to make our God too small.

Because our society wants "the answer," too often we fail to allow for the paradoxes that are a part of spirituality. Spirituality, I believe, is never static; it's always evolving. As we nourish the soul, we'll have many moments of ambivalence, ambiguity, and uncertainty concerning the spiritual life. If we don't, we're probably making our God too small.

Because I'm an ecumenical Christian, my viewpoints and beliefs are colored by that fact, and my viewpoints and beliefs may not be yours. That does not lessen the importance of mine to me, nor yours to you. My spiritual life is built on the belief that God is Love and I am a channel for that Love. As a channel for a power that is greater than myself, a power that transcends life's transitory ups and downs, my life has meaning.

Time and experience have shown me that attitudes and actions which culminate in joy and inner strength evolve only from life anchors that are securely knotted to a spiritual faith. If our attitudes and actions fail to reflect our God, we're not being spiritual. And sometimes, regardless of our personal theology, that's because we're focusing on the letter, not the spirit, of our faith.

I can limit my Christian faith by picking an isolated passage of the Bible, pounding it to pieces, making literal what's symbolic, wringing all essential meaning out of the passage, shaping it into what I want it to be. Grabbing little slivers of my faith, I run the risk of making my God too small.

I try not to run that risk. Rather I find it a full-time, never-ending, daily challenge to live the essential core that underlies the entire Christian religion: "Thou shalt love the Lord thy God with all thy heart, and with all thy soul, and with all thy mind" and "Thou shalt love thy neighbor as thyself." (Mt 22:37–39 KJV) Focusing on this foundation, this essential core, rather than on shards and slivers, forces me to underscore the spirit, not the letter, of my faith. Fortunately, I have a checklist for how well I'm doing: "The fruit of the Spirit is love, joy, peace, patience, kindness, goodness, faithfulness, gentleness, self-control: against such there is no law." (Gal 5:22–23 RSV)

Faith Gives Birth to Hope

Do I always do a good job distinguishing between the letter and the spirit of my faith? Of course not. Will you? I doubt it. I believe there will never be a day when we say, "Now I know the answers. Now I'm a spiritually mature person." Once we do this, we've quit growing spiritually. Because we are, indeed, two-sided, flawed humans, all we can do is *try* to focus on the spirit, not the letter, of our faith. I can tell you that trying brings more joy than not trying; I can also tell you that focusing on the spiritual core of our faith leads to hope.

Not too long ago, a personal crisis pulled me more tightly to my own spiritual core. After I'd had months of bowel problems, my gastroenterologist went on what she called a "search and destroy" mission to find the cause. After days in the hospital, CAT scans and

> ❧ TAKING THE JOURNEY TOWARD SELF-AWARENESS, WE
> ENTER THAT SACRED SILENCE INSIDE US AND FIND THE GOD
> WITHIN. IF WE SAY THERE IS NO GOD IN OUR LIFE, PERHAPS
> IT'S BECAUSE THERE IS NO SILENCE ❧

ultrasounds, I had an endoscopy and a colonoscopy. The night before these tests, I poured out my fears to my paper psychiatrist. Knowing a cancerous tumor was always a possibility, I asked myself what regrets I'd have if I discovered I had only a few more months to live. If something were seriously wrong with me—or if nothing were—I wanted to look back and feel I'd lived my life well.

I typed steadily for over an hour, asking myself if there were nooks and crannies of my life that I wanted to change. What would I feel I'd left "undone"? What regrets would I have? The longer I typed, the more I realized that my life anchors were clear. I had been living my life purposefully; regardless of how the tests came out, I would continue doing so. My life had been, would continue to be, focused on my relationship with God, myself, and others.

My relationship with God influences my relationship with myself, and those two relationships impact my relationship with those around me. The qualities within me—my life anchors—are what count. If they are anchored to my spiritual core, I will have lived well. As I finished typing, I had an inner peace that comes only from hope and faith. When I heard the test results were good, I realized both my physical and spiritual lives were healthier.

This solid spiritual faith which leads to hope gives us a satisfying sense of what we're living for, an assurance that our being alive makes a difference in the world. I'm convinced that until we anchor ourselves to our personal God, we'll remain joyless, bobbing through life, pushed and pulled by whatever current tide controls us. Without this mooring, without this faith, we'll have a hard time handling life's lousy deals.

To ignore the spiritual because we've lost faith in some religion is to deny a piece of ourselves. Major religions agree that the power and presence we call God is within us. Taking the journey toward self-awareness, we enter that sacred silence inside us and find the God within. If we say there is no God in our life, perhaps it's because there is no silence.

Spirituality is an essential component of our beings and must be contemplated and resolved if we are to understand our place in this universe, if we are to find hope for tomorrow. I believe this spiritual faith in a power beyond ourselves is the essential anchor for cultivating wholeness. The hope that grows out of this spiritual faith gives us inner strength. This hope isn't the certainty that life will turn out well; it's the belief that life makes sense regardless of how it turns out.

ADDITIONAL SOURCES

Adler, Mortimer. *How to Speak, How to Listen.* New York: Macmillan Publishing, 1985.

Allen, James. *As a Man Thinketh.* Seattle: The Keenen Press.

Benson, Herbert. *The Relaxation Response.* New York: William Morrow, 1995.

Cousins, Norman. *Anatomy of an Illness.* New York: W. W. Norton, 1979.

Covey, Stephen. *The 7 Habits of Effective People.* New York: Fireside, 1989.

Drummond, Henry. *The Greatest Thing in the World.* London: Collins, 1953.

Frankl, Viktor. *Man's Search for Meaning.* New York: Pocket Books, 1963.

Hammarskjold, Dag. *Markings.* New York: Knopf, 1964.

Jordan, William George. *The Majesty of Calmness.* Westwood, N.J.: Fleming Revel Company.

May, Rollo. *Man's Search for Himself.* New York: W. W. Norton, 1953.

Merton, Thomas. *Love and Living.* New York: Harcourt Brace Jovanovich, 1965.

Moore, Thomas. *Care of the Soul.* New York: HarperCollins, 1992.

———. *Meditations.* New York: HarperCollins, 1994.

Peck, Scott. *People of the Lie.* New York: Simon & Schuster, 1983.

Powell, John. *Happiness Is an Inside Job.* Allen, Tex.: Tabor Publishing, 1992.

———. *Unconditional Love.* Niles, Ill.: Argus Communication, 1978.

Schweitzer, Albert. *Out of My Life and Thought.* New York: Henry Holt, 1949.